Window Pains

A Testimony of Healing

Written by Reverend Tracey Murray

ISBN-10:   1987622596

ISBN- 13:   978-1987622591

LIBRARY OF CONGRESS CONTROL#   12196482651

Copyright ©2018 Tracey McDonald, U.S. Library of Congress

All Rights Reserved. The reproduction, transmission, or utilization of this work in whole or in part in any form by an electronic, mechanical or other means, now known or hereafter invented, including xerography, photocopying, or recording, or in any information storage system, is forbidden without permission of the copyright holder.

All material in this book is the life and thoughts of Reverend Tracey McDonald and has no relation whatsoever to anyone having the same name or names. Any resemblance to actual persons, living or dead is entirely coincidental

Graphic Art/ Cover Design: Cast Me Not Full Service Agency

Acknowledgments

To My father:

I've said before, there are not many who are blessed to have two fathers like mine; the first being God... and the second being you, Mr. Carl Henry Taylor. For that I am truly blessed, you are my muse.

To My Daughter: Kawana Ruby Dillard (Lil Girl) - I love you to life. I can't wait until you tell your story. Your story is the essence of who you are. I love you dearly. To Rebecca and Bri (my other Lil Girlz) - I love you as if you were my own. My story is yours as well as it is Kawana's. Remember to write your own endings. Love you to life...

To My Grandchildren: You see babies; we do come from somewhere, but for me, it started here. I love you.

To the two Cornell's: I love you both more than life...you both have added to me in ways that you will never know, but my Spirit is soaring as a result. I am learning to love totally, and entirely and for you both I have put down my guards. You two will always get the best of me and we together have finally found our forever home.

Dedication to my dad who didn't ever get to see the finisher product, but 2/9/2018 will forever be on my mind, and you will forever be in my heart. I Love and Miss you Dad.

Hey D. Girl, you inspire me to know end. I thank you. Keep shining because you make the world a better place… and remember, *"No More Knockoffs, Real Recognizes Real"!*

Hey Cassandra, thank you for being my friend. To my sisters… you know who you are… Invest-in-yo-self.com and let's expect great things.

I have a special shout out for Mrs. Kathy Armstrong for assisting me with the editing process, and even after reading my book, she is still my friend and for that I thank you.

"Who I've known as "Mama" is dead and now my home has been taken. My school was taken. My teacher was taken. My friends were taken. My bed was taken. My toys were taken. Even my cat, TC (short for Top Cat) was taken! Yes, all that loss, and then I was taken….

Preface

"There are gold and a multitude of rubies:

But the lips of knowledge are a precious jewel."

Matthew 20:15

After many years of being told that I should write a book, the time has come for the book to be written. I've learned during this process that just because you should write a book, and you may even have a book or two inside of your innermost spirit - if it's not time, it's just not time. As the old saying goes, *"...if it doesn't fit, don't force it."* The time has finally come for the birthing of something profound, somewhat healing, and definitely necessary.

I've considered whether or not anyone would be interested in reading this book because it's *"my story"*. I realize everyone has their own story, but not everyone is willing to share the laughs, joys, pains, fears, or depths of who they really are. But I'm transparent, and I've bought into the idea that God knows everything. And He knows everything about me. That has given me the courage to put it down on paper and to share my story with you.

There was an author who once wrote a book entitled, *"I Wouldn't Give Nothing For My Struggles"*. I'm not sure who that author was, but that is now my testimony because really, *"I wouldn't give anything for my struggles"*. My struggles represent me by design and yes I believe that God made me this way. I hope that I am not infringing on any copyrights, but if I remember that this is my first book, so don't sue me yet… at least let me get started.

Trust me, this story has been a long time to come and it's not by chance. It is my experience, but experience none the less. My experiences have shaped and molded me into the person I am today. Who I am is not complete; this book is only part of the story. There are more layers to this story that are stored in my spirit, and they are soon to come, so stay tuned.

I declared long ago that I would write this story when I no longer carried a chip on my shoulder or looked at the world through foggy lenses. The fog has lifted somewhat now and I can see more clearly… though maybe not completely clear. Once I was able to compartmentalize the panes, things became a lot clearer than they were. Now, at least I can write the story with a better understanding of the players and how each and every one of them played the role that they were designed to play to help deliver the masterpiece, *"me"*.

I'm writing this story no longer angry because of the cards that I was dealt. I've come to be thankful for each card dealt, and more than thankful to the dealer! Yes, God dealt those cards and He placed them perfectly. I know this to be true because my life is the evidence of how good of a dealer that God is. This story is simply a catharsis in which I have the opportunity to love where love is warranted; forgive wherever needed, learn to embrace my past, and live my truth today.

To my family and friends who may find my story subjective, I say, that's okay. It's okay because this is my story. And when you write or tell your story, I promise not to complain about the subjectivity of your truth.

I don't remember the day that I decided this story needed to be told, but I do remember the fervor I had when I began writing. It was like God sat me down and placed the pen in my hand. Once the pen was in my hand, the story took off. The story began to tell itself as I watched the pen flow. I became excited with each stroke of the keys that delivered my life on paper. I was awed because it was like God was telling me my story, and reminding me of the things that I had chosen to forget. God was saying, *"No don't forget the past because you are going to need those lessons because your future is just beginning"*. For the first time ever I began to look at my life as part of my destiny and not like an unforgiving curse. Finally, I am in line with God, and I now want for me what God wants, and that is why I wouldn't give anything for my struggles. It was all necessary.

So God made this story come alive.

I understand now God and thank you for my past. I understand that this is my story, but it is necessary to ensure that my only child and my grandchildren know this story because my story is also theirs; my beautiful daughter and her five children will not have the opportunity to meet many of the people I make mention of in this book, well at least not on this side of living, but they were worth knowing none the less. They were our family and as the old saying goes, "family is all you have, you can't choose them, and you can't give them back because God made the connections without our permission.

I know my only child and my grandchildren may sometimes wonder where we come from, children we did come from somewhere. We don't have a long list of relatives, at least not from my side, but what I had I can only share with you the memories. I won't label these memories good or bad, but I will call them necessary experiences. Those experiences are what made up and filled in the cracks of the window panes of my soul and I am forever grateful.

Tracey at the tender age of 7 years old

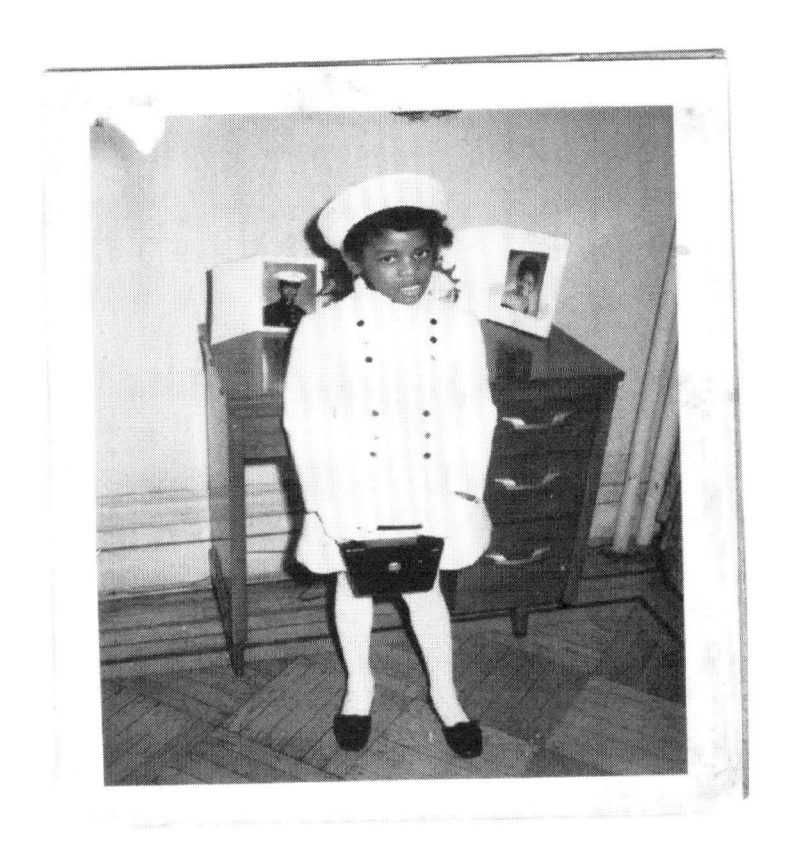

"It's just a hairline fracture"

"Heavenly and All-Knowing God; the Creator of All, the Protector of All, and the most Loving of All. I ask you, God, that you heal the wounds of the past. I ask God that you provide a protective shield over my friend Pat, and the many others that have lived their lives in silent Pain. I pray God that you heal Pat from the inside out and I pray that you heal us from our horrid secrets and give us the strength to endure. I thank you, God in the name of Jesus". Amen

P.S.

God, I haven't' seen Pat in at least 40 some odd years, but if she happens to be up there with you, can you give her some extra molasses for me...

Thanks

The Good Ole Days

As far back as I can remember I would like to think I've been in the pursuit of happiness. I was raised by my grandparents, whom I affectionately called, *"Mama"* and *"Papa"* and they provided me with all of the comforts of home. Mama and Papa afforded me a foundation for life and it is that foundation that has given me the courage to always strive for more, to be more, to want more and to continue to press towards the mark

Yes, it was that foundation provided by Mama and Papa that resurrected my spirit back to life after I had given up and died a thousand times... Yes, I had died in the spirit a thousand times, I was walking among the living, but I was a corpse, dead to the spirit. I won't talk about that I right now because, for now, I just want to talk about the *"Good Ole Days"*. Yes, *"The Good Ole Days"*; the days when I played hopscotch and stickball on my block in the streets of Brooklyn. These were the days when Mama had dinner on the table by six. I could stay out until I saw Papa walking down that long street towards home. He would be just getting off the train from work. I knew then that it was time to come in. I'd have to say goodbye to all my friends because it was time for the secrets of home.

Yep, the good ole days; when we talked together,

laughed together and Lord knows we cried together. The days when Michael Jackson was singing, *"Stop, The Love You Save May Be Your Own"*. The days when I begged mama for that maxi coat because that's what every young girl my age had. The days before I realized that welfare had provided the cheese or that Mama couldn't tell the welfare that Papa lived in the house with us. Yep, the good ole days, when I had to help Mama takes all of Papa's clothes to the neighbors so when the welfare lady checked the closet she wouldn't see signs of a man because we needed that check.

Yes, I remember the good ole days as if they were just yesterday. Papa would bring home a toy from the toy factory, where he worked, and a toy just for me... every Thursday. Yep, I remember, it was every Thursday that Papa would bring good tidings, one for me, one for him and one for Mama. I knew the exact day that he would bring home new toys. I can still see him coming down that long block carrying two packages. One package would bring me joy for hours on end, but the other package... well, let's talk about that later because remember, this chapter is about the *"Good ole days"*.

I remember being loved by Mama and Papa. Mama would show it daily, but Papa's love would only come on the days he brought home the brown bags. Towards the end of the brown bag days, I would find myself hating him and afraid for Mama. Mama was the only loving person I really knew. I didn't understand why he hated her so much. On most days he just hated her silently. But those brown bag would send his hate into action. It was times like those that I would be reminded of songs like, *"I'll Always Love My Mama"*, and I did especially love my Mama on the brown bag days. It would be on those days, and possibly the next few day, that she would need all the love she could get. I tell 'ya, by the end of the brown bag days I found myself hating Papa. However, I won't talk about that yet because this is the good ole days.

I think practically every Black person that lives in New York can trace their beginnings back to the south and my family was no different. I have to admit that I don't have a lot of roots to trace, but I know the planting began in the south on my father's side. My mother's side, well I was never quite sure where they were from. Surely it had to be somewhere in the south. I didn't get to know my mother and her side until much later. All through my life, I would catch glimpses of them; it was almost like looking through a pane, but more on that later. Remember this part is about the good, ole... well, you know the rest.

Ok, back to the South, Mama and I would go to Wilson, North Carolina every summer and boy did I enjoy those summers! Summers free of Papa, Johnny Walker Red, brown bags, and Mama sitting at the window of our second-floor apartment. Mama would be looking out of the window through blackened eyes that I could only see when she would accidentally take her shades off. Yep, Wilson, North Carolina... the land of watermelon, homemade lemonade, fresh peaches, and plenty of sunshine.

These were some roots that I could attach to; good ole Uncle Freddie, and Grandma Minnie. Boy, were these some good ole days! Now I was just old enough to understand that there existed a racial divide. This racial divide didn't have anything to do with white people. It was a huge divide between dark-skinned black folk and their light-skinned counterparts. Yep, we black folks had gone and separated ourselves based on skin tones. This was a little different than what I had experienced back home in New York.

Funny how life goes, we get away from brown bags and black eyes and we run into the great divide. Good thing Mama was light skin because she didn't have to suffer while we were in the South, well at least not as much. Yep, the good old south, Wilson, North Carolina, where if you were light you were alright. But if you were black, you better stay back, and I mean way back! Well, Mama was light skinned so she was alright, but guess where I fell on the color chart? Let's just say I had to stay way, way, way back. I didn't mind though; because Mama was always her happiest being in the south with Uncle Freddie and Grandma Minnie.

Every summer Mama and I would travel to the good old South. I don't remember exactly how long we stayed with each visit, but it always seemed as though we stayed for a lifetime. I was always sad to leave. When we left we would find ourselves once again at the mercy of the brown bags. We won't focus on that though because this is the good ole days. I remember the good ole south and the fun that I would have each summer. There was Uncle Freddie, Grandma Minnie and then later came Uncle Freddie's wife. We won't discuss her right now because as you might know by now, this is about the good ole days.

Wilson, North Carolina, where I was carefree; jumping, climbing, running, exploring, roaming and looking for the next adventure. I must say that having fun in the South was much different from the fun I had in the streets of New York. When I think back, the North was always more intense. Playing was serious stuff. For instance, I recall the times we would play with the ice cream man that came around daily. We would get free ice cream every day... we just couldn't ever tell anyone. You see, in the North, playing sometimes consisted of the ice cream man wanting to be touched in different places. Then the whole crew could have whatever kind of ice cream they wanted. What a game, but we won't talk about that now because these are the good ole days.

Wilson, North Carolina where I was foot lose and fancy-free; where the streets were dusty, the days were long and the Boogey Man was non-existent. Nope, the

Boogey Man never came to the South back then. The Boogeyman did arrive later, but for a long time in the South, I was Boogey Man free. I was always afraid of the Boogey Man. In some ways, I think that I am still afraid of him today.

I looked forward to Wilson, where I had one friend. And boy did I look forward to playing with her every year. Yep, I remember as if it was yesterday. Her name was Pat and she was the most beautiful friend I ever had. I mean, she was light- skinned and had long pretty hair, and she sure knew the value of being light-skinned! Pat really knew her worth. At least she knew that her worth was a lot more than mine. And she let me know every time an opportunity afforded her. You see, I was the exact opposite of Pat. Everything she was, I wasn't. Pat had good hair. I had hard course, kinky hair. At least that was the way my hair was before Mama put that straightening comb and lard to it. My hair may have smelled like a vat of fatback, but it was slick as a can of oil when Mama got through with it. Pat was light skinned and I was Black as coal, at least that's how I saw myself compared to Pat. Pat was rich, and I was poor, she was country smart and I was city slick, Pat was really special!

I was skinny back then and back then skinny didn't really have any value, not like it has today. If I would have known then that people would one day spend millions of dollars on surgeries, diets, liposuctions, and mummy wraps for skinny, I would have bottled mine and been rich today... missed opportunity. In the good ole days being skinny was a curse. There I stood, dead smack in the middle of the good ole days being too skinny, too black, with hair too nappy and smelling like fatback! Wait, had I mentioned that I was blacker than a tire slick, with a nose as big as a fig? Well, at least that's how Pat described me. And I did say my friend Pat was the total opposite, right?

Yes, my dear friend Pat, she reminded me every chance she got that I was too Black, too Skinny, my hair was too nappy and I was just too ugly to amount to anything worth having! Pat really knew her worth and she really knew how to measure the worth of others. Pat was such a good friend. How could I ever have lived without her?

I never told Mama, Uncle Freddie, Grandma Minnie, and certainly not that mean ole Uncle Freddie's wife about the things Pat would say or do. I just accepted what she said as the truth because surely Pat must know. She would come to the house every summer morning to get me to come out and play.

I guess, by now, you've gathered that my friend Pat wasn't much of a friend... but what did I know? During those summers in Wilson, my dear friend Pat would show up every morning to come get me so we could go out and 'play'. I would be waiting with open arms. I was waiting eagerly for the new torture of the day. In the midst of the play and torture, I actually had some fun playing with my friend Pat.

As I think about it now; Pat may have been my first teacher because she did teach me how to endure pain in silence. I was willing to play because eventually I would have some fun. I was willing to wait…. Lesson learned. What's pleasure without the pain right? I didn't know then that I was being set up for an entire lifetime of learning to endure the pain and waiting for the days where I would find a glimpse of pleasure. I never realized, until very recently, that I could have a life that was filled with 'feel good days'. I know the old saying, *"you have to take the good with the bad",* but I spent what seemed like an eternity of enduring the pain to get to the good part. That's all I'll say about that now because, as I've said on several occasions, these were the good ole days.

Ah, Wilson, North Carolina, summers filled with warm molasses and hot buttery biscuits. Now, wait, I know when you think about hot buttery biscuits that you are probably thinking about popping open the can and sticking the pre-made biscuit in the oven. Erase that thought! I'm talking about the biscuits that put flour all over the table. These biscuits involve water, lard, kneading and a rolling pin. I'm talking about having flour the on your nose biscuits! I'm sorry children, so many of you will never have that experience because you weren't back there in the good ole days.

It was in Wilson that I learned to sop a biscuit. You may not know what sopping a biscuit is, but be clear; it's not the same as dipping! *"Sopping"*, as it is more affectionately known, is when you are really getting down to the essence of a biscuit. There is an art to sopping with a biscuit. Please allow me to explain. First, you take that homemade biscuit. Give it a visual inspection as you hold it in your hand. Turn it around slowly, so you can determine which way and where you want to break it off. Once that's done, you smell the aroma that bursts from the now broken biscuit. You look down at the plate filled with the dark brown molasses. Before you put the biscuit down in the molasses, you touch the molasses with your finger (inspecting the texture). Then you gently place the biscuit down in the molasses, carefully holding it in place with your five fingers. At this point, you swipe back and forth several times. Now you have officially sopped a biscuit. So you see sopping and dipping are two totally different experiences. I hope everyone will one day have an opportunity to sop a biscuit.

Yes, it was also in Wilson that I met my first bowl of grits. Man, I'm telling you, these were the good ole days. I know everyone has probably heard the term, *"fish and grits"*. You probably think you've even had some. But let me tell you, there is nothing like the fish and grits of old. There was nothing better on those summer mornings; actually, there was nothing better in Wilson than *"fish and grits"*. It was the fish and grits that helped me to survive playtime with Pat. It was the fish and grits that helped me survive the ugliness I felt in my soul each time Pat reminded me of my blackness. It was the fish and grits that helped me to survive the beatings Pat would put on me for being too black, too skinny, nappy headed with a fig for a nose... it was the fish and grits.

It was in a bowl of fish and grits that I first met God. But I didn't realize until much later the comfort He provided me with something as simple as fish and grits. God always looked after me. I once heard God always looks after babies and fools, and I was still a baby. God looked after the fool later on. You see, it was the fish and grits that stuck to my belly and gave me strength and endurance. It was God that allowed those hot buttery grits to be my shield of armor, and it was the fish that fed my spirit. So with all the things that Pat did to me, my Spirit was continually being fed. And you know, God has used fish to feed his people's spirits before. I'm sure you've read the stories of how God used a couple of fish and some loaves of bread. As quiet as it's kept, I believe God had some Molasses too.

I hope this part hasn't made you sad because I want you to rejoice with me, and remember that we are still in the good ole days. See, we are talking about the panes of life; this is just a hairline fracture and I am okay.

You know, in all of the summers I spent in Wilson, playing with Pat, I never met her parents. Thinking back, Pat was always like the Lone Ranger. It always seemed as though Pat knew exactly when I would arrive in Wilson. She would be sitting on her front porch waiting. But did I tell you I was never allowed to go on her front porch? Nope, Mama wasn't having that... and she meant it.

Pat lived right next door to Grandma Minnie, but it seemed like they lived in two different worlds. Pat lived in an all red brick house with a huge front porch that featured two rocking chairs; but no one ever sat in those rockers, not even Pat! A strange thing about that big, old, red brick house; all the summers I went to Wilson I never met any of Pat's family. It was like she was the only one living there. I'm sorry Pat, but I understand now, better than I ever did... and I really pray that you've been able to heal.

Yep, Pat was the Lone Ranger; with the exception of me in the summer. In retrospect, I think Pat needed me as much as I needed to be there in the serenity and freedom of being away from the brown bags. Maybe in some weird way, I helped her find the worth she pretended to have and know. I realize when we are hurting we often hurt others. Sometimes it is not intentional. It's just all that we know. Over the years I've learned, when people have little control or power in their lives, then we will often gain a temporary reprieve from powerlessness by hurting others. We have learned how to prey on the weak because often times we don't know how to pray for them. But let us pray now for Pat:

Funny, this is the first time I've prayed to God to heal someone from my past. However, I have a feeling this prayer will be the first of many. As a matter of fact, I am sure this will be the first of many prayers to come throughout this story. As you read this book my prayer is that you pray for yourself and the healing of your own hairline fractures. Pray that God fills the cracks in your spirit with his love so you can become whole. Broken pains will keep you bound and open cracks that haven't been filled with the love of God can make you bitter, so take care. There is freedom in healing, but it may cost you something.

I never thought Pat would be so instrumental in whom I was to become. What I know now, but didn't understand then, is that God is a god of relationships. I truly believe each relationship we encounter is designed for a specific purpose. There are no insignificant relationships and we never know when we will be entertaining an angel. I promise to be inspiring to those placed in my path.

I remember Grandma Minnie's house as a white, wooden house. However, the white wood really looked like gray wood. But I remember... it was white. Now I'm not sure, but I would bet a nickel that house leaned to the left, depending on the way you were standing in front of it. Grandma's porch was wooden just like the rest of the house. Man, I got some of the biggest splinters in my hind parts from that darn porch! I sure did love the good ole days... splinters and all!

Grandma's house wasn't big, but it was big enough for me. We even had a parlor where I remember playing by myself most of the time. I would play games that I made up. I played the game called 'swallow the quarter'. Yep, almost choked to death on that one, but I was lucky because Mama saved the day! I remember Mama running into the room and accidentally picking me up by the leg as she missed my arm. Holding me upside down in sheer panic, she caused the quarter to fall out of my throat. Thank you, Mama. And thank you, God. It just wasn't my time.

I was a mischievous kid, so you know there were many butt-whooping's for me! In fact right after mama saved me from the quarter swallowing episode, she whipped my butt. I didn't understand it then, how Mama saved me from choking to death on that quarter and then threatened to kill me if I ever did that again! Anyway, there were plenty of spankings. However, they didn't overshadow the fun during those days. Those whooping didn't take anything away from the fish and grits, or biscuit sopping with molasses... nope, they didn't compare.

I think back to my good friend Pat because she gave me more than a few whooping. Not the kind that mama gave; mamas were love taps (so she said). Pat's, on the other hand, was because I was too black, too skinny, and far too nappy. But even that didn't overshadow the fun I had during those summers in Wilson, in the good ole days.

Yep, the good ole days where there was always life in Grandma Minnie's house, even though she never got out the bed. Summer after summer, and year after year she remained in the bed. I remember the summers when the ambulances would have to come and she would just ask to not have the siren on when they were on the way.

What was it, Grandma Minnie? Did the sirens remind you of something bad; was it fear of dying? Why didn't you like the sound of the siren?

I tell you, those good ole days were streaked with the fractures of life I've yet to understand. That's okay because they were good ole days none the less. I always looked forward to the food, fun, and freedom I found when we went south for the summer.

"In all your ways acknowledge Him, and he will make your paths straight"

Proverbs 3:6

Let us pray:

Father God, in the magnificent name of Jesus, I thank you for loving me and I thank you for healing this brokenness. God, you are Merciful. Father, you created me, and I know you created me flawlessly. God, help me to always see myself the way you do. Father God, help me to see my good. God when you created this earth you looked down on the 7th day and saw that your creation was good. Your creation was good then, and it continues to be good. God thank you for providing me with Grace and Mercy, thank you. God provide me with the sight to see through the window panes of your spirit. I want to see behind the veil as I walk slowly to your altar.

I pray, God, right now for the Spirit of Forgiveness. Lord, I ask that all strongholds be broken from my life and the life of all those now in bondage. Father, I release all of my hurts to you as I no longer carry the weight of bondage, strife or pain. Father God, you have all power in your hand, and I know you can do anything. Thank you, God for turning my crooked paths straight and God. Thank you for Brooklyn.

Amen

A Letter to Brooklyn

Did I ever tell you, Brooklyn, why I had to leave so soon? Brooklyn, did you even know that I was gone? I never told you about the loneliness I felt all those days and nights after I left. Somehow, I just knew we would never see each other again. I didn't even have a chance to say bye. Whatever happened to all of my friends? Did you keep them safe in your streets? Did they survive? I missed you, Brooklyn. I missed everything about you. Did you miss me?

I missed the long walks I use to take on your blocks, remember? We use to walk everywhere. I missed the smell of your alleys and the rush of your streets. I missed the noise, yes Brooklyn, most of all I missed the noise.

I missed your heat, Brooklyn. I missed the way the steam used to come off the streets when it was really hot outside, and then God would send a shower. We used to say when it rained and the sun was still out that the Devil was beating his wife. Was that true?

Brooklyn, I think it's time we talk about why I left. I will begin by telling you I never wanted to leave you, I loved you. I didn't have a choice... my very first experience of powerlessness. I was bound by circumstances... I was helpless. I was afraid, and you... you couldn't help me. You were too busy moving, shaking, buzzing; I guess just being Brooklyn. Or maybe, you were just giving me a way out.

Do you remember it was in you that I first learned to play the childhood games children no longer play;

Mama May I? Hopscotch, Skully, Double Dutch... I refuse to explain these outside Brooklyn street games. Red Light, Green Light, 1-2-3. I would run just as fast as my 5-year-old legs would carry me. I was always the one that got caught though. I always believed they cheated; but Brooklyn, only you know the truth.

Do you remember the *"Johnny Pump"*? Looking back I would guess the Johnny Pump was the poor folk version of a swimming pool, (but we weren't poor) LOL! It would always happen on one of those hot days, Brooklyn; when the streets were steaming from the heat of the sun and someone would bust open a fire hydrant. Oh how I would beg mama to please let me get wet, please, please, and sometimes she said yes.

Red Rover. Red Rover send Tracey right over! I loved it. But even then I had a hard time breaking through. I know that you young children probably don't have a clue as to what I'm talking about. Google it!

Do you remember when I lived on Carlton Street? The street that was right around the corner from Cumberland Hospital? The street where I got my first pair of Go-Go boots! Remember how proud I was to own those boots? They were boots just like the ones the women that lived there wore. You remember the Go-Go Boots!

Do you remember the house across the street from my house on Carlton Avenue? You have to remember it Brooklyn; after all, the house was on one of your streets! Well anyway, a lot of women lived in that house. They wore short pants, big Afro's, and Go-Go boots! Mama didn't like them very much. There were a couple of those women that were my friends. You see Brooklyn; even then, I was sometimes lonely. When my friends couldn't come out to play, I would sit on my stoop and just watch the women that lived across the street. I would think, 'One day, I will be just like them. They were always smiling, and seemed happy... and they wore Go-Go Boots'!

The women that lived across the street on Carlton became my friends and sometimes they would even come and sit on the stoop with me when Mama wasn't looking. Boy, were they beautiful? And they had a lot of different boyfriends. I would watch as their boyfriends came by and took them in the house. They would never stay for long. They were always in and out like grease lighting! Mama didn't like those women very much, there were a couple of those women that were my friends.

As a matter of fact, Brooklyn, it was one of those women that brought me my first pair of Go-Go boots. I remember begging Mama, *"...can I keep them, Mama? Mama, can I keep them!? Please?"* Well, she let me take them in the house. But to this day, I don't remember what happened to those boots. I guess they were going, going and gone.

Funny how life happens though; it wasn't long after that I watched as cars full of police kicked in the doors of the house across the street. The women and a couple of their boyfriends were taken away, and I heard Mama say, *"Good riddance"*. Mama didn't know I was secretly hoping that I would one day see my "other' Mama while I was sitting on that stoop. I hoped that she would one day come to that house looking for a little girl. I hoped that one of those ladies would tell her about me. Doesn't the Bible say something about hope?

I didn't get to tell them I couldn't find the boots

they gave me; the boots that Mama said I could have. Brooklyn, I didn't get to thank them for not minding that my hair was nappy, that I was skinny, and that my nose was big as a fig! Just like you and me, Brooklyn, I was separated from those ladies and I didn't even get to say goodbye.

That's okay though, I'm not mad. I've learned, Brooklyn that every Goodbye ain't gone, and every distance doesn't have to be far. I learned that on my own!

Do you remember Cumberland Hospital around the corner from Carlton Ave? Of course, you do, you're Brooklyn. Anyway, that hospital was like a monument to me. I walked by that hospital almost daily. It was the biggest building that my five-year-old eyes had ever seen. I guess even then it didn't take much to wow me. I am still easily impressed. Actually, I was impressed with the building until I had to spend so much time inside of it!

I had asthma, Mama had sickle cell and together we were a sickly crew. But I wasn't as sick as Mama. Mama never really told me what the disease of sickle cell was all about. I just remember the effect it had on the first woman I ever loved. I remember the days and nights she used to blackout. Yes, that's what they called it, blacking out; whatever it was, it scared me to death.

I was always watching Mama to make sure she wasn't about to have another one of those blackouts. Blackouts made you fall down without warning; made you lose control of your body, moving all around in quick jerking motions. Every time mama had a blackout I thought it would be the end. Each time a blackout occurred, I thought this time she wasn't coming back.

One particular time when I was about 5 years old, Mama had a blackout. She fell out and her body twitched really badly! I didn't know what to do! I was powerless. It took many years before I was able to find my strength. Mama would have these blackouts, and people would start running to get spoons. Other times people would scream. *"Don't let her swallow her tongue!"* They would stick the spoon in her mouth. Mama would jerk and jerk, and jerk, and jerk, and then she would stop. There was a lull, but the jerking would stop... there was a lull.

Brooklyn, you weren't much help back then, but that still wasn't a good reason for me to leave without saying goodbye. That still was not a good reason... yes, Brooklyn, we spent enough days at Cumberland Hospital. Mama and I were a sickly crew.

Do you remember all of the times I had to travel your streets to get to that same Cumberland Hospital? Do you remember all of the times I was afflicted with asthma attacks? Do you remember when that German shepherd police dog got me? I taunted him while he was chained up. Week after week, month after month, I taunted that dog, until that dreaded day when he finally got a hold of me. I don't know if dogs believe in payback or revenge; but when that dog did get a hold of me, he was not playing nice. Bad dog! Bad dog!

It was during one of those stays at Cumberland hospital that I learned something else about me. I learned that not only was I too black and too skinny, and that my hair was too nappy and my nose too big. I learned from a little old white nurse that I was a monkey and deserved to be behind bars.

You see hospital stays were different back then. Or were they only different if you were black and poor?

Well, I don't know, but I remember being in the hospital to have my tonsils removed. Mama said my tonsils were the reason why I kept having asthma attacks. You see Brooklyn, it wasn't because of the dirty streets, or the fog in the air. It wasn't because of the lead paint on the walls! I just needed my tonsils removed.

One time I was really sick after the asthma attack. I could not leave the hospital until I had my tonsils removed. After this emergency surgery, I wasn't able to eat solid food. So what does the nurse give me, Brooklyn? You got it! A glass of milk. Well anyone who knew me and was worth their weight in salt, knew I could not drink milk. I guess during those days they didn't keep charts on Black folks. Maybe no one asked about allergies and things that make you throw up.

Well, I was forced to drink milk, I threw up all over my bed, even between the hospital baby bed rails. I vividly remember that day, sitting in that bed on my knees holding on to the bars. The bed was like a regular baby bed, made out of iron with a very thin mattress. The bed had very tall bars which were either used for my protection to keep me from falling out or going AWOL. I had a bedpan in my hospital prison bed. I was very sick, crying, and shaking the bars of that bed. As I was peering out between the bars, a white nurse walked by. I cried out for help. The nurse looked at me and said, "Look at that monkey". I think my heart stopped that day. It was on that day when I understood why I was too black and too skinny, my hair was too nappy, and my nose was as big as a fig. It all boiled down to one fact. I just wasn't good enough. In my five-year-old mind, I had declared war. The war would be internal; it would be long, hard-fought and dirty. This would be a war that would take 40 years to fight and it would take many hostages along the way. This war would kill a spirit on site; yes my spirit was sure to die. This was the day I became different, and different wasn't anything good.

You see Brooklyn; I have finally learned how to release the things of the past that held me bound. I hope that this helps you too.

You remember when Papa gave me the nickname, Monkey? That was one of the greatest terms of endearment Papa ever used on me. I was his monkey; not because I was too black, too skinny, had hair too nappy, or even because my nose was as big as a fig. Nope, it wasn't any of that. He called me *"Monkey"* simply because he loved me, and that was as close to a term of endearment as Papa could get.

Brooklyn, why is it that Papa could call me "Monkey" and it is such a term of endearment, but that old nurse lady called me *"Monkey"* and it would leave me fractured somewhat like broken panes in a window? Why was it Brooklyn, that I believed the nurse and not my Papa?

Now that I think about it Brooklyn, maybe she didn't mean anything by calling me a *"Monkey"*, or maybe she did. At this point does it really matter? Maybe what matters most at this stage of my life is that I no longer allow others to determine who I am. Maybe what I will become is bigger than I can even imagine. Maybe, the great *"I Am"* created me as I am and he left it up to me to see through the broken panes. He may have left it up to me to see, but He didn't leave me alone.

I know you realize there were many more things that happened on Carlton Street. I know you remember it was on that street I first learned to ride a bicycle. Remember Papa holding the bar on the back of that two-wheeler, Brooklyn? He held it until he couldn't hold on any longer, and it was time to let me go. That's the funny thing about life though, we hold on and hold on until it becomes apparent it's simply time to let go.

Brooklyn, it is time to let you go and I will, but I have many more stories to tell. Thank you for loving me, and then spit me out. I love you, Brooklyn. I hate how we ended without saying goodbye, but I'll say goodbye now, Brooklyn, because that loving part of us will never return.

"For everything, there is a season and a time for every matter under heaven."

Ecclesiastes 3:1

Johnny Walker

There's a season and a time for every matter under the heavens; I get that, but how do I get prepared for those things that are to come. I know there is a biblical scripture for everything, and every situation, but God, was there a scripture for the *"Brown Bags"*?

Brown bags were significant, but not nearly as significant as the contents which went by the name of Johnny Walker. Yes, Johnny Walker was a sly devil wrapped in a brown bag. Johnny always came in a long bottle, Papa called it a fifth. He was reddish brown inside of his bottle and his aroma was strong. Johnny was almost like a genie in a bottle because his results were magical. Yep, in a blink of an eye or a nod of the head, Johnny would change the atmosphere from cheering and laughing to screaming, crying, bloody noses, and black eyes. Maybe Johnny wasn't a genie, but he sure was in a bottle.

I was always fooled by Johnny, week after week, believing this time would be different from the last time. Maybe I just needed to believe Johnny would be different. I didn't know or understand that he couldn't be anything other than Johnny, vile and destructive.

Johnny Walker was a smooth talking devil who always knew the right words to say to Mama and Papa. He would say those words at just the right time. I bet I wasn't the only one in the house that thought Johnny would be different week after week. Yep, he always started out good in our house with the laughter, long and short stories of old.

Johnny was friendly and he seemed really innocent at first; sitting in his brown bag, not bothering a soul when his lid was on. He almost always came on Thursday because that's when Papa got paid. I remember those days vividly. Papa would proudly walk down the long road to home, holding his head high. I would be the proudest kid on the block, seeing my Papa with his brown bags.

If I was outside when Papa came home, I would immediately turn to follow him up the stairs. I would always be eager to see what was in the bag for me. I already knew what was in the other brown bag... that was for Papa.

Papa would get his glass from the cabinet as we would sit down to eat our dinner. Although we always ate dinner together, we only talked to each other on Thursday. After dinner, Papa would bring out the records and we would dance to songs like, *"It's Your Thang"*, boy; would we dance. Papa always said I knew how to boogaloo, but on Thursdays, he could boogaloo too... and so could Mama.

I would always leave the excitement and joy and go into my room to play. Even at my young age, I had learned that the excitement was only temporary. I had come to know Johnny and I was no longer fooled by him disguised in that bottle.

I learned quickly that Johnny Walker contained in the brown bag would eventually turn on you. You see, it really wasn't the brown bag or the contents that were the problem. It was everything that happened once the lid was twisted off the bottle.

Mama and Papa would be drinking and dancing. I would be dancing too, at first. I had learned to watch the facial expressions and body movements of others. I would see how quickly the smiles would turn to frowns, accusatory stares, name calling and then the fist, the hitting, and the screams. There used to be a song that went, *"Smiling faces, tell lies, and they don't tell the truth"*.

Johnny Walker Red and Johnny Walker Black, they always came in a fifth because that was the way Papa liked them. Either of the Johnnies would be poured over ice in our best glasses, bringing short lived celebrations! Every Thursday, I waited for Papa to come down that long street with those brown bags in his hands, one for him and another for me!

There were some days though, on special days, that Papa would take me to the store with him to pick old Johnny up. I even remember the old liquor store where Johnny used to hang out, waiting for the unsuspecting.

Papa and I would sometimes go to that old liquor store together. I would hold his hand while I skipped, skipped, Skipped to my Lou, right beside Papa. Sometimes on the way to pick Johnny up, Papa would buy me a lollipop, a coconut-pineapple ice with a slice of pizza or my most favorite, a glazed donut. You see, going to pick up Johnny was such a treat for Papa that I could almost have anything I wanted. Most of the time, on Thursdays, Papa came home with Johnny already in the bag. Papa would have one brown bag for him, and one brown bag for me.

Johnny made Papa so happy that sometimes he would take me, Mama and Johnny out visiting friends and relatives. Papa knew lots of people that liked Johnny too, but I think Papa liked Johnny most of all. Somehow it seems as though he gave Papa more courage and helped him to talk more. Most of the time, Papa was a quiet man. He was just not a man of many words; however, Johnny put a lot of words in Papa's mouth.

Papa wasn't much of a fighter either... until he got into a fight with Mama. He would always beat her in a fight. Every time we went out to visit and took Johnny, a fight was sure to break out. Johnny would always make Papa remember stuff that happened long ago. He would get really mad, and the fighting would begin.

I don't know why Papa would always listen to Johnny Walker, but I stopped liking Johnny way before

Papa did. Actually, I don't think Papa ever fell out with Johnny like I did.

I learned to be afraid of the brown bag, but I was more afraid of Johnny. You see, even though I was a child I could see Johnny for who he really was.

How did I get from those good ole days to here? Sitting in the window, watching and waiting, and thinking;' it's going to be better this time'... I will save her this time! Maybe this time he won't be so mad... Mama, if you could just cook the dinner the right way. Please, Mama, don't say anything back when he yells at you. Mama, do what you always tell me to do, you remember Mama. Repeat after me, Sticks and Stones may break my bones, but names will never hurt me! Say it Mama please, and Mama, please don't drink out of the brown bag.

Johnny Walker Red and Johnny Walker Black always came in a fifth. The two Johnnies would be poured over ice in our best glasses, and boy did they bring the celebration! Every Thursday, I waited for Papa to come down that long street with those brown bags in his hands, one for him and another for me.

We would play records on the stereo. I remembered one of my favorites was a song by Stevie Wonder, *"Signed, Sealed, and delivered";* and another, *"I Just Want to Celebrate"* (Another Day of Living). There were so many good songs that I can't remember the names of them all, but boy did we dance. Well, we danced until the mood changed. The dancing songs would go off, and then he would play the sad songs. 'Don't play the sad songs Papa because they always make you cry. Mama, tell him not to play the sad songs, please Mama, tell him not to play the sad songs.' Mama would say, *"... go to your room baby, just go in your room and don't come out."* 'But Mama, I don't want to go in my room. Can't we dance some more, sing some more songs, don't play those sad songs, Papa, because they always make you cry.'

Screaming. Screaming. Screaming. Please stop. Don't kill my Mama! I was afraid, I was helpless and I wanted to die. Not to avoid her pain, but to avoid my own fears. I hated Brown Bag Thursdays because they always made me cry.

I was so afraid Mama was going to die. I mean, she already had those blackouts that I didn't understand, but now she was taking beatings for reasons I couldn't possibly fathom.

'Please don't kill my mama!'

Have you ever been so afraid that your body would freeze, stiff, refusing to move? I mean afraid to the point that flight wasn't an option, even if it was to save your own life? I would hear the slamming of doors, crying, and furniture moving. Running, screaming and bad words... bad, bad words.

I would hear the banging and the screaming for long hours as I lay under the cover so afraid; the only thing I could ever think or say, quietly in my mind, was *"Hey Papa, please don't kill my Mama."*

The next morning Mama would go about like nothing had happened. I wondered why after those nights Mama would have dark glasses on the next day. Yes, she had dark glasses that she mostly wore on Friday's.

'Mama, why did you stay?' I remember sitting in the window with Mama as she rocked back and forth; waiting, waiting, on what I still don't know. She said she was waiting on Jesus as I watched the tears roll down her cheek from under those dark Friday Morning sunglasses. She sat in that window rocking, waiting, waiting, and rocking, and waiting. She said Jesus was going to fix it, but I wasn't so sure. I was angry with Jesus because he never fixed it.

Most mornings Mama would walk me to school and sing songs to me. My favorite was the Mocking Bird Song. She would say, *"...hush little baby, don't say a word."* As if I was the one crying! Mama, I wasn't crying, you were. I was simply afraid. I was afraid for you. I was also afraid for me because I always wondered what I would do without you. How would I live? I was afraid for you Mama, but I was only a little girl and I couldn't keep you safe.

Mama, I know in your song, you said, *"...hush little baby, don't say a word"*, but it was in silence that you wept. It was in silence that you had tears streaming from your blackened eyes. It was in silence that I watched you have those blackouts. It was in silence, Mama, that we would believe this time it would be different.

A letter to God:

Dear God, I am praying for my Mama. God, I know that to be absent from the body is to be present with you in the Spirit, but I didn't learn that until much later, and I really missed my Mama. God, I think I understand why you took her, but at the time I didn't understand why you left me. You see God, I needed her and I was sad when she left. Jesus, you never came or maybe you did and I just missed you. God, do you remember what happened that day, the day she left? Well, I remember quite well. That morning I woke, I remember Papa and Johnny had a long night the night before. Papa woke up feeling angry as he always was after a night with Johnny. He was really saying mean things to Mama. Do you remember? I sure do. Mama walked me to school that morning with tears in her eyes. Boy, it was one of the mornings that Mama sure needed some extra loving. I remember God, 'because I was in the 2nd grade. I thought I was big enough to walk myself to school because I knew the way. But Mama would always walk me to school and she would always be waiting for me at the end of the school day. On this day, she wasn't waiting for me. I waited just as she always told me. I remember God how she would say, *"If you ever come out and don't see me here, you just wait for me because I'm coming"*. This day God, she didn't come and it was getting late. But I knew the way home, so I walked home by myself. I was going to surprise her and I knew she would be proud of me. I told her that I knew the way home. God, you remember Mama didn't open the building door. I rang, and rang, and rang that bell so hard until the upstairs neighbors let me in. I went up to our apartment on the 2nd floor, but the door was locked. I had to go upstairs to the neighbor's house where I stayed for a couple of hours. I always did like the neighbors. When they sent me downstairs to see whether or not Mama had returned home, our front door was open. I walked in looking for my Mama and found her face down in the bathtub. Mama was dead! She was lying face down in the bathtub, God! What was I supposed to do? I was only a child!

God, my Mama was gone. Now, I know this may sound a little selfish, but God, I needed her to stay so she could love me. There were so many things I didn't have the opportunity to tell her. I never told her about the ice cream man. You remember the Good Humor man that use to come on our block every other day with the *"Good Humor"* Ice Cream Cart. He would always be dressed in all white and be as friendly as he could be. He would give us all ice cream if only one of us would touch him in places where he wanted to be touched. He would always choose Alexis. I wonder why he always chose her. Alexis was the biggest of us all. And she would do anything just to have us like her. It was sort of like me and Pat when I went south for the summer. Gee God, when you think about it we capitalized on Alexis' need to belong somewhere when the whole crew of us were actually misfits. I think the ice cream man knew it and that is why he wanted to be touched in certain places. I bet he knew we would never tell because he always came back to our block. God, I never got to tell Mama. But could you ask her not to be mad?

God, I never got to tell Mama how we use to go to Pratt Institute right down the street. We would play and run, and oh, what fun we had. Yep, the ice-cream man knew we would be there too because he would always meet us there. I remember the biggest secret of all when he had the blankets in his cart, and he and Alexis were under those blankets on the ground just rolling and rolling around. You know God, I don't remember whether or not he gave us ice cream that day, but Alexis sure was crying. She told us we should stick her in the butt with a safety pin to prevent her from becoming pregnant. I never got to talk to Mama about those things because she was just gone too soon.

"For I will show him how many things he must suffer for my name's sake"

Acts 9:16

Taken

Through the eyes of a child, she called it taken. Yes, everything that I ever believed, or trusted was simply snatched from under me.

My mama was taken. My home was taken. My school was taken. My teacher was taken. My friends were taken. My bed was taken. My toys were taken. Even my cat, TC (short for Top Cat) was taken! Yes, all that lost, and then I was taken.

There were people all around, everywhere. I remember every room in our house was packed with people. I heard them say, *"Poor Tracey, what's going to happen to her now?"* Well, I was wondering the same thing. I watched as people were deciding what of Mama's things they wanted; things they would remember her by. Well, how was I going to remember her? I kept hearing the voices saying, *"What's going to happen to Tracey now"*?

I never thought I would be taken! Why couldn't I stay? Mama, why couldn't you stay? Where are you taking me? I don't want to go! Wait, why isn't Mama moving? Why is she in that box? Are you going to put her into that hole in the ground? What will happen to her when it rains? What if it gets too hot? You know Mama has those blackouts! Is this real Mama? Are you really not coming back? Save me, Mama, because I don't know what to do next. Mama, you have always loved me, but who's going to love me now? I'm scared and I don't know who to trust. What about all those songs you sang to me? You told me you would always be my Mama, well where are you going? Who is going to comfort me now? I keep thinking about all the days you loved me, and all the good times we had. What about the secrets that I kept? You never told me that one day you would be gone… and that I would be taken! I don't want to go Mama; I don't want to be taken!

Mama, I promise I won't be scared of the brown bags anymore. I just need for you to stay. Please Mama, next time I will wait at the school just like you said. I promise next time I won't walk home by myself; I'm going to learn to listen just as you asked Mama, but please don't you leave.

That was the cry of a little girl that was about to be thrown into the abyss of the unknown. I was the wide-eyed little girl searching through a sea of faces; looking for the reassurance that I always found in the face of my Mama.

I had never been so scared in my life. After all, I thought to live through the brown bags, the blackouts, and the fighting was the worst it could have ever gotten. Nothing could have prepared me for the death of my mama, and what was to happen next in my young life.

Before they could put Mama in that cold, cold

ground in Wilson, North Carolina, there was fighting, arguing, and blaming. There were also some secrets that were discovered and mysteries that were to unfold. There was also one constant that I had learned to hate by this time; that was Johnny Walker Red and his cohort Johnny Walker Black. They were right there in the middle as they had always been.

I remember just being numb and silent as I continued to search the faces of the adults around me. I was among adults that acted as though I wasn't in the room, as they planned my abduction. There were the adults that would listen to Johnny Red and Black, but never to a child that was crying out in anguish. Nope, the child's pain could never make them feel how the Johnnies made them feel. I do believe during my Mama's death and funeral I had my one and only out of body experience. I watched me sitting there, trying to talk, and I even saw my lips moving, but no one could hear me. They only listened to Johnny.

I'm packed, but Papa can I please stay? I won't walk home from school by myself anymore, and I'll clean my room when you tell me to. Please Papa, Please Papa, let me stay, don't make me go. I don't want to leave, Please Papa, Please.

Now I am in the back seat of the car, and I don't even know who's driving, I don't want to know whose driving, I don't care whose driving, it's not you, Mama. I was looking out of the back window as we drove down that long Brooklyn Street; our apartment building kept getting smaller and smaller until I couldn't see it anymore. I couldn't see my Papa anymore. I couldn't see my friends anymore. I wondered did any of this matter to anybody except me. Did anybody tell my friends that I was being abducted? Did anyone tell my teachers or my classmates? Did anyone tell the ice cream man that I wasn't coming back?

I can't explain the insurmountable grief that I felt during this period in my life; the degree of helplessness, powerlessness, hopelessness that I felt. I almost spent a lifetime trying to heal the wounds of the loss of my Mama. The lessons that I learned through this experience were far from healthy; living many years later in a constant survival mode. I learned that love, don't love anybody, and it sure doesn't last forever. And it really doesn't matter why love leaves; it just matters that you understand it doesn't last forever.

I learned that goodbyes are often gone forever, and closed eyes may never open. I learned that love isn't always enough, and giving all you have can still leave you lonely. I learned to never depend on people to do what they said they would do.

I learned that I could never be loved again by anyone because I would never belong to them as I belonged to my Mama. I learned that Papas that used to love you won't love you anymore when Mamas are no longer around.

I learned that it's not important to say goodbye... just leave, it's the best way. I learned not to have too many friends, so you don't have to feel bad when it's time to leave them. There will always be a time when you have to leave them.

Please understand I am not claiming these lessons to be my values today. Well, at least not all of them. What I have described were the lessons that were taught; not only by what people said but also what they didn't say. I learned from everything that happened after Mama left.

Mason Jars

I watched a movie once in which the main character's wife died, and he was stricken with such a sense of sadness that he went to hell and then heaven to find his wife. The state of sadness I felt took me, *"the little girl"* to a hell I couldn't have returned from on my own. It was only His Grace that brought me back, but it took a while. Does it have to take 40 years for everything? I was broken hearted, overwhelmed with grief and I didn't know what to say, what to think or how to act under this circumstance. *"I just wasn't prepared"*. I had learned how to survive the brown bags, the screaming, the black eyes, and the fear. But God, you had not prepared me for the Mason Jars of the South.

I wanted to fight, but I didn't know with whom? I wanted to scream, but no sounds would come out when I opened my mouth. I wanted to cry, but tears were useless and they only burned my eyes and then my face. I would remember a song that Mama would sing when I would be sad. The song went like this, *"You are my sunshine, my only sunshine, you make me happy when skies are gray, you'll never know dear how much I love you Please don't take my sunshine away"*. Did you really mean that Mama? I don't know what happened or why you left, but what I know is that you wouldn't have just left me because I was your sunshine.

I was left with an uncontrollable grief that was fueled by anger. And self-loathing wasn't far behind. I can't really explain the events that happened next, but *"I just wasn't' prepared"*.

Out of all the things you prepared me for in our short time together, you didn't prepare me for how to live without you. But could you have ever prepared me for that? Could you have prepared me for the things that were to come? I bet you didn't even know about the *"Mason Jars"*, or maybe you did? Maybe you thought I would never have to know about Mason Jars?

Mason Jars and the death of my Mama changed my life forever.

Whatever happened to the fairytale that said little girls were supposed to have *"Sugar and Spice and everything nice"*? Maybe they didn't know that in the south? Maybe all they knew had been forgotten because nothing was as important as the Mason Jars of the south. Yep, Mason Jars would personify the transition from North to South, and boy did I receive a hearty welcome.

I understood I was now living in the South and the dynamics had changed. The pain no longer came in *"Brown Bags"*, but it came in clear Mason jars. I can almost smell the licorice scent of the contents of the Mason jar. There wasn't any more Johnny Walker Red or Black, but they called it *"White Liquor"*, some even said it was *"White Lightning"*, but regardless of the name that they gave it.... A rose is still a rose.....and the rose still has thorns.

It seemed as though Mason Jars had consumed my new living quarters, and everywhere I turned there it was. *"White Lightning"* they called it, liquor by the pint or by the jar, but however it was consumed it was dangerous. I watched as my new living quarters became consumed in the pleasures of its misery one swallow or gulp at a time.

Things had changed now. Remember Mama when you use to say, *"things can turn from sugar to S&%$"?* Well, I was dead smack in the middle of the *"S&%$"!* A whole community affected by the contents of the Mason jar. I guess *"White Lightning"* was true to its name because what happened next was pretty damn quick! My brown bag Thursdays was nothing compared to the Mason Jars' everyday blues. Yep, *"White Lightning"* they called it!

Well, I guess the transition from North to South wasn't all bad. I made some friends, and I lived with loving family members, well they loved until... you know who came over! You guessed it, *"The Mason Jar."*

"White Lightning" and Mason Jars was the pillar of our community. *"White Lightning"* wasn't even disguised; nope there wasn't an elephant in the room, hell, we all knew it was there.

Every other corner house was a liquor house, but that was okay because at least now I had some friends. I needed some friends because I just needed to be loved once again the way Mama used to love me. I would spend a lifetime looking for Mama's love; I use to be her only one.

I had to adjust to some different things in the south. I had made some new friends, but it seemed as though we spoke a different language. For instance, I would say *"Park"* and they laughed. They would say, *"Playground"*, and I thought that was quite funny, but it was okay because they were my new friends.

They called me *"proper"*, and I called them *"country"*, but it worked out.

I will never be able to explain why I always found the group of misfits, probably because I never fit, but I always fit with the misfits, yep, we were one of a kind.

We were one of a kind in more ways than we even knew back then. We all heard the screams and witnessed the beatings and pretended like, *"that doesn't happen in my house"*, but in reality, where we were living, it happened in everybody's house. Just as soon as *"White Lightning"* that lived inside of the Mason jars would enter in, everyone was in danger. Yes, it happened in almost everybody's house. *"White Lightning"* was my new normal.

We would all just meet at the park they called a

'playground', and sit in silence until someone would say that old familiar line I had said for many years, *"please don't kill my mama"*. See, I told you we were more alike than different. We were misfits in a community that didn't know how to save its children. We were misfits in a place that was prone to black eyes, bottle beatings, Mason Jar drinking, liquor house slinging, all night dancing, and the stench. There was a stench that belonged to the long nights of *"White Lightning,"* cigarettes, and violence. On many days we would be called from our playground to come and clean up the aftermath of the party they had had the night before. We were called to clean up after parties that we weren't invited to or to the party to show some drunken grown-up the latest dance. It wasn't like we wanted to attend either because we had our own parties going on, but I won't talk about those.

    I knew that I was misfits because I had lost the only woman in the world that ever loved me, and that I had ever loved. Now that I think about it, I loved Mama like Jesus, *"I loved her because she first loved me"*. Yep, Jesus knew me first and she came right after, she knew me, and with all that she knew about me, she loved me.

    I had figured out that the loss of Mama's love was my cause for profound sadness, but I never could figure out what great loss my living quarters had suffered. They had to have lost something important because the whole community was pretty sad. Now, I don't mean they walked around every day like zombies, but there seemed to be a blank stare in their eyes. What were they missing I wonder?

Had they suffered such a great loss that it could only have been consoled by the contents of the Mason jar? Yep, *"White Lightning,"* as they called it, the Consolation Bureau for the lost in Spirit, and the broken-hearted.

Well, at least I had some new friends, and we would sit in the park they called a 'playground', and try to act as if we weren't misfits, in a place where nobody seemed to fit.

I remember the fun we would have... sometimes, almost and in many ways like the *"good ole days"*. Mama wasn't there and neither were the brown bags, but boy did they have their Mason Jars.

We were big enough to run errands. We were often sent to Tic Tocs, the neighborhood grocery store, where we could buy anything from a nickel's worth of cookies to a pound of hamburger. These were the days when your word was all you had and most of the time all you needed to get a little credit from Tic Toc. We could run up a tab at Tic Toc's and because I was big enough, I went to Tic Toc's almost every day to run up the tab. I ran up that tab with Reese's cups, pickles, penny candy, and whatever else I thought me and my fellow misfits needed. I still don't know how my aunt found out about me running up that tab. I just know she found out and when she did, she kicked my little butt from an Amazing Grace to a Golden Opportunity! Needless to say, I wasn't running up tabs anymore. As a matter of fact, I think I stopped liking pickles, Reese's cups, and penny candy all together... well at least for a while.

For a very long time, I couldn't go back to Tic Tocs; but I didn't want to go anyway because I think he (the shopkeeper) was the one that could have eventually told. Maybe she found out when it was time to pay the tab; either way, I didn't want to go back to his neighborhood store.

I might have been banned from Tic Tocs, but there were several other locations I wasn't banned from and frequented regularly.

I was also allowed to go to the house on the corner. I always went with very strict instructions like, *"Go to Mary's and get me a pint, and take this Mason jar and tell her to fill it to this line. Tell Mary I know I owe her, but give me $2.00 worth and I will pay her on Friday".* I would then get that last instruction that went like this, *"... and you bed not drop a lick!"* Dropping a lick of the contents of that Mason jar could get you beat unconscious... or at least into the next week, whichever came first. We may have dropped a lot of things, but what we didn't drop was that $2.00 worth of *"White lightning."*

We were a mischievous bunch of misfits that

learned the spoken and unspoken rules of the quarters in which we engaged.   We learned that children were to be seen and not heard, and that grown folks don't lie. So if a grown folk told something about you, it was the truth. Then the other grown folk would whoop ass, and that's just the way it was. The grown folks would call us chaps. I never quite knew what a chap was, but I knew that our role in the quarters was to be seen and not heard. Mama taught me children were to be seen and not heard, but it appeared this same rule applied to the chaps.

I learned through the Mason jar value system that grown folks don't lie. Well, that may have been the truth, but that damn *"White Lightning"* never saw a truthful day in its life. *"White Lightning"* would tell a lie in a New York minute, but we were in the south. On most days I had to learn and understand with whom I was dealing. I became a professional in handling the *"White Lighting"* because the grown folks always left me in the care of the Mason Jars. I had to pull from my experience with the brown bags, but it worked

I learned valuable lessons and almost all of the lessons taught me how to lie, cheat, manipulate and steal. I didn't really understand those lessons back then, but what I did understand was that my survival was more important than ever now. You see, what happened in the brown bag days was kind of different. It was different because no matter what happened during those days I could depend on Mama and Papa to take care of me.

    Mason jar days had no such loyalty and anything was subject to happen...

Once There Was a Man....

He lived on the corner in the liquor house. I use to see him all the time when I dropped in to pick up the pints, or the $2.00 worth. The man also had another house; I remember... he had keys. Sometimes he would take me and one of my best girlfriends to the other house, right after he finished his *"White Lightning"*. It was okay for us to go because grown folks don't lie, right?

I was the look-out and I took my job seriously. I monitored the door as he and my friend would enter the back room. I can sometimes still feel the chill of that house. It was always very cold in there. I suppose that was why the man and my little friend would get under the covers.

I would watch through the peephole, the only thing I could really see was him on top and her on the bottom. The cover would be moving; going up and down, up and down, and up and down, faster then slower, faster then slower, then faster again, and then stop!

He told me I would get a badge of honor because I was to be the keeper of the secret. I kept good secrets back then and I was the only one who knew he and my friend would go up and down under the cover in the bed in the other house that he had keys to. Yep, he would give her a dollar and make her split it with me; because I was such a good keeper of the secret. Nope, I never told and I thought I never would.

One day to my surprise as I was sitting in the park they called the 'playground', I was all by myself. That same man, the one that lived in the liquor house on the corner, came by. He asked me to go with him to the house around the corner. Was I happy that I knew how to keep a secret? After all, I was, almost grown! I was all of 10 years old and I wouldn't have to split my dollar! Grown folks don't lie... right? He said it was okay for me to do this; he had spoken to my aunt. There would be no further need for me to tell her. And he would have a dollar waiting for me at the end.

He put me in that bed, took my bottoms off. He tried as hard as he could to go up and down once the covers were over us. It just wouldn't work! He tried to put that thing in my mouth, but I didn't like that, so he made me leave! I still had to be the keeper of the secret or else!

How was I to know that going up and down under the cover was to be so painful? My friend never told me it was painful and after all, we were both ten... hell, we were almost grown! He didn't give me my dollar. I had done my best. I tried to do what he said; after all, I had watched him and her several times. I thought I knew what to do, but he made me leave and he didn't give me my dollar! Now, I had another secret. And that was, *"I wasn't good enough to get the dollar. I could never tell anyone; not only was I not good enough to go up and down under the cover, but also I wasn't even worth the dollar."*

"Who shall separate us from the love of Christ? Shall tribulation, or distress, or persecution, or famine, or nakedness, or peril, or sword?"

Romans 8:35 KJV

Moving On

"I don't remember why I had to go, but then again, I don't remember why I came. It was somewhere deep in the places that you can't see that God touches your soul and allows you to be free. I've been told that freedom isn't free, but I know what it feels like to be trapped so if this is as close as I can come to freedom then I will take it. I'm moving on!"

Leaving

Wow! So it's time to leave again. Can anyone tell me where I'm going this time? So you mean I have to leave... and not come back?

Did I do something wrong? I promise I'll be better? Don't you want me here? Didn't you say you loved me? I mean, I know I am not your little girl. And now that Mama's left, I really don't belong to anybody. Please don't make me leave again. Don't you understand I am holding on for dear life? Do you not understand that I am trying to figure out where I fit?

Where am I going? Wait, don't touch my things! Did you find out I wasn't worth a dollar? Did he tell you? I thought it was a secret!? I mean…. I tried! Where am I going? Don't you want me anymore? I have friends here! Don't I fit?

So I'm leaving again. Will it always be this easy to give me away? Will anybody ever want me to stay?

Leaving again without my permission; does anyone ever ask a kid that is almost grown (I am 10), whether or not she wants to move again?

I wonder, will this move be different or will there be more brown bags… or even bigger mason jars? Did someone die? Okay, that must be it; someone must have died, but whom? Will there be playgrounds and more liquor houses? Will I have friends? Will they like me?

I didn't like my living quarters, but I had adjusted. I knew the rules of engagement. I knew how to become invisible, how to keep secrets. I could go to the store by myself and how to run up a tab. I knew the difference between a pint and $2.00 worth.

No longer was I bothered by the screams and the beatings in the night. Didn't I always wake up in the morning and act like everyone else, acting as if nothing happened the night before like I hadn't heard the screams? I acted as if I didn't see your black eyes like the house wasn't torn down. Yes, I acted like I wasn't scared, and I never told anyone what happened in our house. Didn't I do right?

I know I had a little trouble in school, but I took the medicine they gave me. Was there something else I could have done? I just didn't want to leave again. Not because everything was so perfect. I wanted to stay because I couldn't predict what would happen at the next place.

You see, when you are living the game of survival, it's always best to be able to predict what's coming next. In the game of survival, change is constant and your square is round. Nothing remains the same and that's a hard situation to predict. So you see, I didn't want to stay because I liked it so much; I was just afraid of leaving.

"I realize that every time someone leaves, they will have to end up somewhere because nowhere is just not a place."

Tracey McDonald

Broken Pains

I don't even remember packing a bag, or getting my favorite toy, or taking anything that would comfort me along the journey.

I just remember feeling broken as if something inside of me had shattered into many little pieces like slivers of glass.

I couldn't tell anyone I was afraid and that now I missed my Mama more than ever. I couldn't tell anyone that I was angry because I didn't want to leave. I couldn't tell anyone that I just wanted; no I needed things to be back to the way they use to be. But, which way was that? It seemed as though the only constant changed. I couldn't tell anyone about my feelings because they just wouldn't have understood, so I kept quiet. I suffered on the inside way down deep where even I couldn't reach. I suffered so deep in such a forgotten place it would take years for me to reach that place, and even longer to heal in that place.

They say you don't miss your water until your well runs dry... well by now I was dying of thirst. I would have given anything to see Papa walk around that corner with two brown bags again. I would have done anything to hear my Mama sing that song again: ... "It's yo thang, do what 'cha want to do, I can't tell you who to sock it to".

I wished I would have stayed home from school on the day my Mama died in that bathtub. Maybe I could have died with her. I would have given anything to not feel the broken pains of my heart.

I remember when Mama and I use to sit looking out of the window of our second story apartment building. Mama would say she was waiting on Jesus. I sat just waiting because I didn't know who Jesus was back then. I remember Mama would wait longer and look harder in the mornings she woke up and needed to wear the dark sunglasses.

Funny thing though, I didn't know Jesus back then, and I was really angry with Jesus, but I found myself waiting for him too just because Mama did. If Jesus was good enough for Mama to wait on, he was good enough for me! I always loved my Mama, 'cause she was my favorite girl.

I have new digs now and this time there were more children that actually lived in the house. And there was soon to be one more on the way. I was a little older now or did I just feel older? Well, I knew that I was the oldest of the other children in the house. Again, I found myself trying to find my place, simply trying to fit. I tell you since I lost my Mama I spent a lifetime afterward trying to find my place and fit. I don't know why finding my place or fitting in was so important, but when I look back I understand now that I just didn't like being me. I didn't like being me because I thought there had to be some major imperfection in me to have caused these major events in my life. I mean, was it that I was still too Black, my hair still too nappy, or that my nose was still as big as a fig? Would I ever be worth keeping? Was it that easy to send me away, to discard me; would I ever be worth the dollar?

My new digs... Now I was lost in the house where I lived. I mean, I knew where all the rooms were, I knew the exits. I got to know the people that shared the house with me, but I was still lost in the house.

Being 'lost in the house' may seem strange to you, but you have to understand how this could happen. You see, your house is the place that contains your soul, the very essence of who you are. Through many life experiences some pleasant and other experiences not so pleasant, it seems as though without direction you can lose your way, kind of like being, 'empty'.

I was beginning to mourn lost relationships, and I had become overwhelmed by grief, but it was all in the inside, down deep in the lost places of my soul, my house in which the Spirit rests. I really missed those brown bags because with all of the trouble those bags represented at least they were predictable.

It seemed as though my life had become fractured and frayed like an old window pane in an abandoned building. I was the abandoned building. I was the window pane that had been detached from its original structure. It felt as though my soul had been laid amongst the debris and thrown out with the trash just like an abandoned window pane all shattered and broken in places. I was the unwanted, broken and detached, lost... I was in need of recitation. I needed God to blow life back into this Spirit.

Yes, leaving will always land you somewhere, and that is exactly where I landed, somewhere! This time though, I even had a title, and they called me 'sister'... sometimes. At other times, I was reminded I really didn't belong; I didn't fit because I just came from somewhere. I was reminded that I was a stepsister, and a 'step' anything is simply a false sense of being.

I spent many years trying to understand the meaning of 'step', and although I didn't like what it represented it provided me with a starting place to finally understand my existence. I began to understand my place and accept my role.

I come to understand that step was the second cousin to 'foster'; which I would become several years later. The term was *"foster child";* in my mind step and foster represented something that was unreal, made up, a substitute, not natural and never belonging.

I came to understand that no matter how hard I tried I would never be the first love. I was fighting a losing battle because neither step nor foster could ever be loved first. That was just unheard of.

I watched from corners as I would be overlooked, and listened as I would be talked about. The 'real' children would always come first, and I guess that was exactly how it should have been. The real children you carried, and then birthed! You grabbed them as they entered into this world. You counted their 10 toes, and then their 10 fingers. You cooed with them and then rocked them to sleep. You rushed to their bedside when they had bad dreams. You had high hopes for their future, so why wouldn't they come first?

I understand now far better than I understood then because I was only a child trying to fit in. I was a misfit trying to fit into a foster situation, and I was always a step away from where I needed to be.

Something was changing here and I wasn't sure what it was, but something was changing. It was the atmosphere for sure. It was something about this place that was always dark even when sunlight was in the room. It was my daddy that was taking me to my new digs. Yep, my daddy brought me to this place. He had provided me with the siblings that constantly reminded me I was a 'step'. The woman that was the mother of my new found siblings wanted me to call her 'Mama', but I couldn't call her Mama. That title had only really belonged to one person, but that person had died, floating face down in the bathtub.

Quiet as it was kept, she reminded me I was fostered as well. It never failed when she got mad at my daddy, she was mad at me as well. I didn't care though; it didn't matter if she was mad at me because of him. I just wanted to be good enough to stay. I was just tired of leaving and leaving had much more effective than just a chapter in a book.

This living situation worked out for a while, but I got introduced to something that was fairly new. I had been hanging low, hiding out, getting along and fitting in... just trying to survive. Now I had to survive something else. I had to survive the whooping's! I know some may think that every child will get spanked from time to time, but even now in my adult mind, I never got spanked! I got my ass whooped, beat, and sometimes my ass was just plain kicked! I apologize somewhat for the language, but there simply isn't another way to explain the experience.

You see, I was the oldest child in the house and I became responsible for the younger child... that's typical family stuff, right? Well, if one kid did something wrong, I would be the first to get my ass whooped, beat, and sometimes I got my ass just plain kicked!

I must say though we were beaten as a team if one got it, we all got it! I would get it the worst each time because I was the oldest and was supposed to know better! Bull*&%$, how do you know what you were never taught? And first of all, I was never taught how to watch bad ass kids that were always reminding me that I was a 'step'. How do you know better when you have only known survival for the better part of your life? The rules were always changing. How was I supposed to know that these kids were now my responsibility? I had never taken care of anything before, with the exception of TC (top cat), but he was taken. Every chance that kid got they would remind me that I was fostered, not real, and just a... step.

We weren't the only ones getting the beatings though. The lady that I couldn't call Mama was getting beat pretty bad... and on the regular. It was kind of sad back then because once again I was powerless. Once again I would hear the screams in the night, but this time I didn't endure the screams alone, we all heard them.

The children that had somehow become my responsibility would be angry at me as if I was doing the beating. I wasn't doing the beating, but because the aggressor and I shared the same blood I would be held responsible. Those times would just widen the great divide. I understood they felt helpless, but did they understand that I was just as helpless? What was that song again Percy, *"When a Man Loves a Woman"*?

I learned something different about love, way different from what Mama ever taught me. See, I knew my mama loved me with everything she had and in his own strange way, I knew Papa loved me too... even though I was in competition with his brown bags, and it seemed as though the brown bag would win on most days, I knew he still loved me. What I learned about love though was that love was very painful, and it was never here to stay. Love couldn't compete with the Brown bags, and it didn't have a chance against the Mason jar.

It seems as though my life had been consumed by what I know now as a false sense of reality. My life had been consumed with Brown bags, Mason Jars, and men that loved to hate women.

Love was a strange emotion that meant something different in each new place I landed. Yes, Love was a funny type of emotion and love taught me this one valuable lesson. You might be familiar with this famous saying, but this is what love taught me and it goes, *"the same things that make you laugh will make you cry."* You know that saying is even in the Bible? That is the most real statement I have ever heard.

As life would have it there came another move, but this time we had to move as a family, and nobody was able to bring anything for comfort. I don't think we had anything left to get once the fire started.

This time everybody had to move, but this move wasn't by choice. It was just that this time I didn't have to move alone. Thank God, because that may have been just too hard for me. We owe this move to one little boy that came to be known as my brother. I won't call his name, but 'Hey Baby Brother'. Remember when you burned the house down? I don't remember all of the details, but I do remember the place was called *"'Double*

Oaks" back then. Remember Baby Brother, you were always getting in trouble for playing with fire, and I do mean always! I wasn't mad at you though, I never liked those digs anyway! We were too crowded in those little rooms. I remember those dark brown, wooden walls… uggghh! But those were our digs back then.

I don't even remember getting a 'whoopin' for the house burning down. Maybe it wasn't my fault and there wasn't any time to whoop. Maybe there was just time to leave. The funny thing is that I don't even remember where we went. I just remember we couldn't stay there anymore. As I stated in the beginning, *"every time one leaves they have to end up somewhere"*. We are moving again, but this time I am not the only one leaving.

"Funny, nothing poetic comes to mind and there are no rhymes or lyrical flows when it comes to this place."

Tracey McDonald

Brick Yard

If moving had taught me nothing else, it taught me not to get settled in any one place because everything is static.

At any time, any moment and without my permission, I could be made to move again and that wasn't by choice, but just the way the cards had been stacked. I don't remember moving here, I just remember getting here. I suppose none of that really mattered now that I'd arrived.

Ironically, out of all the forward motion that I had made with all of this moving, I don't ever remember packing or unpacking. I just remember landing, and now here I was. Maybe remembering packing or unpacking wasn't important because I knew I wouldn't be staying long.

This was my life, and I had learned early on to just accept what is, without question. My life was truly unpredictable… at least I couldn't predict it. Was I being punished for something?

I wish I could say this move was better than all of the others, but I can't say that. What I can say is that this move was different. Yes, the *"Brick Yard"* was a different kind of place. It was a heavy place. In retrospect, the Brickyard was blanketed by poverty and consumed with self-loathing. But I didn't know that then. In the Brickyard, there was always the hustle and bustle of life. Everything and everyone moved with what seemed to be the pace of a locomotive. The only problem was that no one seemed to be going anywhere. We were all standing still.

The brickyard was very crowded and the roaches provided little room for anyone else. I don't remember ever seeing roaches until I moved here. And man, was there an infestation.

I wasn't sure about this place because something just wasn't right. You know how you get that 'ain't right' feeling deep down in the bottom of your being? I use to hear some of the grown folks use the word *"hankty"* to describe people that were shady. That would be exactly how I could best describe this place. The brickyard was Hankty, to say the least.

I guess because I was a kid back then I wasn't supposed to notice, but I've always been super sensitive to my surroundings. The Brown Bags and Mason Jars had raised me that way.

This was another place where I would find myself a misfit again. Just like in the 'living quarters', I wasn't the only one that was a misfit. In the Brickyard, it was as though nothing fit, and nobody belonged. It was simply designed that way.

Mason jars were always prevalent in the Brickyard,

but that was okay because I knew what to expect from Mason jars. There was something else that was prevalent also. I couldn't quite put my finger on it until after I had been there for a while. There was something in the air, or maybe it was something that could be detected in the faces of those that lived in the yard. Everybody seemed to be in motion, but it was slow motion at a fast pace. It was almost like everybody was 'lost in the house'. There was something in the air and the people in the brickyard were victims of it. There was still the usual fighting, anger, and women getting beat... the regular Mason jar norms with which I had become accustomed. But there was something different in this place. It was almost like time was standing still. I just couldn't put my finger on it, maybe I wasn't supposed to.

The struggle was different in the Brickyard, and there was a different look in the eyes of those that lived here. I couldn't call it then, but I knew intuitively that I was amongst something like the walking dead. There was a sense of hopelessness in the Brick Yard; I guess that's what poverty brings.

In the Brickyard everybody had a hustle; in fact, everybody needed to hustle because I think everybody was hungry.

Everybody was hungry in their spirit. It just seemed as though their souls were empty, something like broken panes.

It seemed as though the children in the house where I lived were always hungry as well. We were hungry for food and starved for attention. Remember the earlier lesson that we chaps learned, 'chaps should be seen and not heard'? It was still in effect. This wasn't the type of atmosphere where we discussed feelings, where the parents encouraged us to express ourselves. This just wasn't that type of party. The only party happening here was album covers and white lines; they called the white lines, *"Horse"*. Now that was a strange name, but I guess the white lines did take them for a ride?

The Brickyard was a true first for me. Although I had experienced a lot of things in my young life, I had yet to experience hunger due to the absence of food. If nothing else, I was always able to eat, until now. I knew how to handle my starving soul because I learned to pretend and I perfected the blank stare. I didn't know how to keep my stomach from growling, and it just wouldn't shut up. Nope, I hadn't experienced hunger until I moved into the Brickyard. We always had a scheme to get fed. Most of the time we were on scavenger hunts just to eat. I started eating and liking mustard sandwiches! If there was nothing else in the refrigerator; there was always a jar of mustard and most of the time there would be some white bread.

I remember that we would sometimes have leftover cornbread. We would put syrup on the bread, a little butter and we would make a meal. I tell you though, that cornbread and syrup were far from the molasses and biscuits in the 'Good Ole Days'. In the 'good ole' days,' the molasses and biscuits were, always made with love. In the Brickyard the cornbread would always be old and way past the expiration date; and the syrup, well, it was just syrup and there was no love intended. Both meals were filling: one filled your stomach, but the other would nourish your soul.

In our house, there would always be fish fries or a chitterling strut. There would also be hot-dog, chicken, and hamburger sales, but we (the children) were always hungry. I never did understand that and maybe I never will. But that's okay because we all survived. Death seemed to be all around us, but none of us died of starvation!

Yes, the brickyard taught me brand new experiences that were far more than I had become accustomed to. I thought Brown bags and Mason Jars had given me all of the life experiences I would ever need. How could I have been so wrong? How was I to know that my past experiences were only a sample of what was to come? Actually, my past experiences provided me with the necessary skills to handle what was to come. I've always heard, *'what doesn't kill you will make you strong'*. They should have called me "Hercules".

The lessons learned in the 'yard 'would impart in my

life for years to come? The Brickyard had new tricks with lasting residual effects on everybody that lived there. Even to this day, the effects of the brickyard continue to linger. The Brickyard has since been torn down, but they can't tear down or tear out the devastation that was caused. Yep, the Brickyard is gone now, but I still see many of the souls that were lost and not all of us are walking dead. Some of us survived, and many of us can be found today sitting in a room saying, "Hi, My name is____, and I am an___.' "

In the Brick Yard, we were all there thrown together sort of like crabs in a barrel. Just like a barrel isn't the natural habitat for a crab, the Brickyard wasn't a natural habitat for us. We were a bunch of misfits trying to find a place to fit and we had found it in the Brickyard. I think we were just happy to have a place to call home. At least I know I was happy or maybe I was just excited because I was not alone.

It was like someone was playing a cruel joke on us in the Brickyard. It felt as though we were thrown together to see who could or would survive in this bricked in hole of a place. This hole was never designed with our survival in mind. It was just a place to put us.

It was in the Brick Yard that I witnessed robberies, murders, break-ins, fighting, stabbings, and so much hatred. I learned to stuff whatever I witnessed, and whatever I saw I knew not to tell. I was already good at not telling because I learned early on. *'Good Humor'* had taught me that. I don't think we hated each other, but whom else would we take out our frustrations on? We were all that we had.

This was definitely a different kind of living here. I must say the grown-ups were getting stranger and stranger by the minute. It seemed as though grown-ups taught me different things depending on my location, but the lessons were never the same.

I guess that's the role of the grown-ups; to teach and train us, children. Doesn't the Bible say something about *"bringing up children in the way that they should go?"* Maybe they didn't read the Bible or at least they hadn't read that part because they weren't teaching me which way to go. Actually, I was lost, confused on the journey, and sometimes when I have flashbacks, I can still be a little unsure.

I had to take a totally different approach to talking to these grown-ups. I almost had them figured out. For instance, I liked to ask them questions when they had just come out of the bathroom. During these times I could almost always get yes for an answer. Case in point, I ask a question and they simply nod yes and I could almost do anything my little heart desired, with their permission. I really liked to ask them things when they were nodding and holding a cigarette at the same time. They would never drop the ashes, but that didn't matter to me. I thought these grown-ups were magic, but now I know they were just high. Me being the misfit that I was started spying on them, and I would always catch them in the bathroom with socks and belts tied around their arms.

I thought these grown-ups had the best magic tricks of all; I mean they would tie a belt around one arm, hold the belt with the other, take the orange cap off the needle, and stick themselves all at the same time, and even with their eyes closed! Magic!

Yes, the Brickyard was different and it was the first place I had ever experienced hunger. Now don't get me wrong, in our house, there wasn't much magic being performed. In our house, they were only making lines with white powder on top of album covers. There wasn't much magic in that, but there were still plenty of Mason jars in our house. Maybe this was different because at least there were bottles with names on them and it was called *"vodka"*. This time the liquor house wasn't down the street but the candy lady was though. The liquor house was our house.

I was a long way from those Brooklyn streets. I was a long way from Papa, and Mama was dead. I couldn't trust these new grown-ups to take care of me because they rarely did. I tell you what though, they had the discipline part down pat. Nope, they never lost sight of how to whoop us, and because I was the oldest I still got it the worst because I was always responsible for those other kids that I never asked for.

This poem was written as a result of the great love and respect that I have for my father. I realize what is meant by humble beginnings, but our beginnings were far from humble.

To My Father

You are like *"Air"* to me because I need you to breath.
You pump air into my spirit and stir my creative soul,
You are my muse and I love you with all of who I am.
You have held me up and have always reminded me that I was created for more, for better, for good.
You have loved me when I had the strength to love myself... and when I didn't. You pushed me on the days that I stopped pushing because I was tired.
People are not often lucky enough to have the love of father God, and the love of the natural father that was assigned to them by God.
I have been blessed to no measure because I have both.
My promise to my father is that:
From this point my life will reflect the love that my Fathers have shown me,
My life will reflect that creative, free Spirit of peace, love and wisdom,
Because that is what my Fathers have given me.
God gave me to you for a time such as this
And everything that we've ever experienced was to shape us,
To mold us, and to grow us to the place of love in which we stand now.
So go ahead and enjoy your day, because God isn't through with you yet.

Your Assignment,

Me

Endings

Brickyard living placed everyone in very close quarters. Our apartments faced each other, only divided by very narrow pathways. We lived in close quarters in tiny apartments that had floors that were black and made of steel. The walls were so thick that we would never hear the neighbors next door unless they were screaming exceptionally loud.

The brickyard didn't provide many choices about who your neighbors would be because, as I said, we were just 'thrust together'. We were so close that we had no choice but to be in a relationship with each other, in one way or another. Each row of tightly knit apartments was filled with some strained relationships, and others not so strained. Everybody went to everybody's house for a cup of sugar, or a stick of butter at one time or another. Everybody ran to everybody's house because in their house a fight had started at one time or another.

Everybody got into a fight for some reason or another. There was always something to squabble about in the Brickyard. It didn't take much to start a fight. We were always fighting for non-existing values. Really when you think about it, what were we fighting for? Funny how the Brickyard had made us all equal, but we didn't realize it then.

Maybe we were fighting because we were so crowded. Maybe we just needed space. Maybe we were just scared that we would be stuck in the brickyard forever? Of course, you know the mason jars and vodka bottles were always present, and they will always lead to good fisticuffs.

I had friends though and yes, we fought too. We fought because the grown-ups had taught us that way of life. I don't know if they meant to teach us that, but we learned it from them nevertheless. Just like the grown-ups we would put somebody's eye out one day, and be friends with them the next in the Brickyard.

I had friends from one end of the yard to the next. My friends and I walked to school together in the mornings, and we came home together every afternoon. We shared our pennies and our dimes so we would have snacks every now and again. We made up dances together, we cried together, and just like in those other 'living quarters', we talked about what went on in everybody else's house while denying what would go on in our own.

After a while in the brick yard, I was no longer a 'step' or 'foster', I just was. After being around for a long while I just became part of the yard with no explanation necessary. After a while, no one asked where I came from or how I got there or who my mama was because that just didn't matter anymore. Even in our house I just became one of the 'chaps', and after a while, I was even receiving equal treatment. Funny thing was that even though I began to feel like I belonged, there was a part of me that would not allow me to surrender to the entire process of belonging. I was always on guard for instance... I never could get my mouth to form the word Mama and attach it to the woman that learned to care for me like I was one of her real daughters. Even though she said I could call her Mama, in my mind that word 'Mama' only applied to one person and she was dead.

Papa and I even connected again and he began sending me gifts on Christmas and on my birthday. For the first time since the death of Mama and even with all of the dysfunction that continued to surround my life I started to feel as though I was at home. I wasn't bothered by the fighting because that was the way of life. The brown bags or mason jars weren't an issue because I had accepted them a long time ago. I didn't even care about the white powder on the album covers or the belts tied around the arms of the grown folks. I didn't care that the grown-ups were nodding and falling asleep during mid-sentence. I didn't care about the beatings or the violence because I had learned this was just the way it was. I didn't care that there wasn't any food to eat. I didn't care about the mustard sandwiches I had to eat because finally, I was at home. What I cared about more than anything in the world was that finally, I belonged somewhere. I had a woman that I couldn't call Mama, but she was good to me. I had sisters and a brother, and a father that would come around sometimes... this was home. Resist as I may, I couldn't deny the fact that I was at home.

Yes, I had a daddy that would come around sometimes, but boy when he came around we all knew it, and he would always leave his mark. I mean literally, 'He always left his mark'. Truth be told, we were happier with his departure than his arrival. His visits were very rarely pleasant, but I was still glad to have him come.

We would always be on alert for my daddy's car to pull up. Everybody in our little cluster would give out warning signals if they saw his car coming before we did.

Yep, when he came around somebody was going to get a butt-whooping', and it wasn't only the kids that would get beat. Many days it would be the butt of the woman that I wouldn't call Mama that would get the whoopin'. It was always a scary thing to watch as he would take her into the bedroom. Sometimes she would go willingly and there were other days when she would be dragged into that room. We would hear the door slam and lock, the yelling and scream, and then the beating, and again we were helpless. It seemed as though every instance reminded me of death. Just like when Papa would beat Mama, I would always feel as though this would be the day she would die.

I always felt so sorry for her because when it was

over she would be so broken, and she seemed so fragile. The scariest of all in my young mind back then was that every time afterward that lady would want to take a bath. I would always think just like I found Mama, dead; in the bathtub, I would find this lady dead in the tub as well. I always associated the deaths with the beatings, and then the bathtubs would be associated with the deaths.

I hated my Daddy for being the one that did the beatings, yes, I hated him for that.

Although I hated my daddy for beating the woman, I would also suffer from survivor's guilt. I would feel guilty because I was thankful it was her and not me this time. I always knew when my Daddy pulled up somebody would be getting a whooping that day. I just didn't always know who it would be.

We lived like this for many years until the last time he pulled up. That last time I remember the lady that I wouldn't call Mama wasn't at home. But we had a babysitter. I don't remember all of the details, but I do remember my daddy had taken all of her clothes and every other thing that belonged to the babysitter. My daddy placed all of her belongings around the tall Oak tree that stood in front of our apartment. I watched as he poured the fluid and set the fire to all of her belongings. As always everybody turned to me as they reminded me that once again my Daddy had made it bad for everybody.

It didn't happen that same night, but it wasn't shortly after that incident that my Daddy came back to our apartment and told me to get my things. Yes, I remember having to pack that day, and then I was gone. Yes, life as I knew it had ended. My friends, my sisters, and my brother would no longer be. The lady that I couldn't call Mama would no longer be around and the life I had grown to know, accept and love was finished.

Hello Brooklyn

Hello Brooklyn, I'm back and so many things have happened since we were last together. Brooklyn, I thought that I would never be back in your boroughs, but here I am. I can't say that I missed you because I didn't think about you much. I am sure glad to be back and under a different set of circumstances.

My father said that I could go back to Brooklyn. I think that he said that I could go back because since the pregnancy and the abortion we weren't the same. We didn't know what to say to each other anymore. It was like we each carried our own amount of shame and guilt for what had taken place. I think that by allowing me to leave we could both have a break from our feelings. Because seeing each other every day was draining us, we didn't know what to say next. He really tried. I think that for the first time since I had known him that my father had given up. I left my father in a bed of regret and doubt, of whether or not he had done the right things to and for his little girl. 'Yes daddy, you had done the best that you could with the little that you had.' There had been boundaries that were crossed, and I believe that he could no longer look at me as his little girl. I had been violated in more ways than one in his eyes. My daddy, my protector, felt as though he had failed. I knew that because I could see it in his eyes. I told you that I was grown, way beyond my years. And my years had taught me how to identify pain and failure. My daddy hadn't failed me, but how was he to know that at this very young age I had already experienced more than most.

I think that my Daddy knew that I was somewhere on a crossroad between womanhood, while still being a child. It was time to let me go.

I wasn't forced to have an abortion; I just wasn't given a choice. As I look back now, I think that my father had to let me go; because making me stay would have been too painful for him, more painful for me. He let me go because it was time. I think that he realized that there were things that he just wasn't equipped to teach me. It wasn't because he was a man that he couldn't teach me, but because there was still so much that he just didn't know.

So now Brooklyn I am back and ready for new lessons, and Brooklyn you were always a great teacher. I was living with my Aunt Pat. I learned to love my Aunt Pat almost as much as I loved 'Mama'. Aunt Pat was my favorite. Even though she has been dead for many years, I am still in love with her.

It was a whole new ball game this time. I was older and had a lot more experiences than I had before I was forced to leave the first time. I had one aborted baby under my belt. I had tackled brown bags, Mason jars and I thought that I was a woman now. Yes, Brooklyn, I was back with a vengeance. Regardless of what I was back with, I was back.

I had relatives that were really my relatives; cousins, aunts, uncles, another grandmother and they all were really my relatives. We had the same blood running through our veins and they actually knew the woman that had birthed me because she was related to them. The woman that birthed me was real and I wondered could I now stop making up the imaginary woman. You see somewhere in my mind I had imagined that there was a woman that loved me so much that it was killing her that she couldn't be with me. I had imagined a woman with a love that was so strong for the little girl that she left that she would be somewhere broken in pieces. I even imagined that one day I would rescue her from her guilt and shame of leaving me and I would tell her that it was okay and that I understood. That was just imagined though, it was only imagined.

Being back in Brooklyn this time somehow brought this woman to live, she was real this time. I hadn't had the opportunity to actually see her, but somehow living here with Aunt Pat made her existence real. Now it's not that I had never seen her because I had. I just don't remember a lot about being with her, spending time.

I remember one incident when I was around 5years old. I was living with Mama; this woman had come to get me. I remember being in this place with her. I don't know where it was or how we had gotten there. I remember being thirsty while we were there and seeing a glass of water on the table. The glass of water was filled with syringes, but I was thirsty. I had asked for water several times. I went to that table and picked up that glass of water; took the syringes out and began to drink. I don't know what made me grab that particular glass, but I think it was because everyone else was focused on that glass. Well, needless to say, that I got everyone's attention at that point. They all screamed at me not drink that water. After that incident, there weren't many more times that I had actually seen my birth mother. Being in Brooklyn this time made me feel closer to her as I searched the faces of these relatives looking for some resemblance of what she looked like.

Truth be told, I needed to have the woman that birthed me in my life. I needed her to explain what had happened to me and why. Somehow I felt as though she knew. I was hoping that she would be able to make some sense out of everything that had happened. I needed her to give meaning to my life because my life had lost its meaning. Once again, I just existed. I learned much later in life that it was her own addiction that had caused her to not be my real mama, but only my birthing mama. I learned later that my birth mother lived most of her young and adult years addicted to heroin and anything else that would make her feel normal. I never got to ask her what ailed her, or why her life turned out the way it did? I wonder did she know what ailed her. There had to be something really bad that would make her put needles in her arm for most of her life. There had to be something that would make her want to spend most of her adult life in bondage and behind bars.

I know that there are very few animals in the animal kingdom that don't protect and keep their young. I know that it is an animal's instinct to protect their babies and fight to the end to protect them. So, what would make my birth mother give me up?

I wonder whether or not she had a clue?

I was happy to be back in Brooklyn, but being here didn't make me feel as though I belonged. I know, that I said I was happy to be back, but even though I was happy to be back, there was an emptiness that I felt on the inside. I had crossed to bear that I hadn't even realized yet. Why is this life filled with so many crosses to bear, lessons to learn, and does every cross have to be so heavy?

Jr. High School

NO PUN INTENDED....

Yes, I am back in Brooklyn now and I think this is where I've always wanted to be. I'm living in the projects and as happy as a kid in Toyland. It just seemed as though I and the projects were a fit, just like the hand in glove. It seems as though I've always wanted to be in the projects, a place where there was no expectation of greatness. The projects weren't designed for us to get out. It was just another brickyard, another day in the neighborhood.

It was a place where I could hide out. If I failed in life, that would be okay. Nothing was ever expected of me anyway. I've always been afraid of failure, but looking back, I think that I was just as afraid of success.

I was never quite sure of who I should be or who I could be; but in the projects, it never mattered, because just like in the 'brickyard' nobody ever expected much. It seemed as though I would always gravitate to areas and people that lived in 'quarters', where everyone suffered from decline and disrepair. I fought hard to live in lack because that is where I found comfort. That is where I wanted to be left.

This time I would found myself living in Farragut Projects in Brooklyn, New York. I think that it was once said that, *"...the projects were designed for working families."* Well if that were true, it must have been the working and still poor families. Because it seemed like everybody was having a hard time living. I believe that I had decided that I didn't want to ever work because working at a job just seemed to make you poor if that makes sense. It seemed as though the more people worked, the less they had... and the more they needed. That was just my opinion. I was on the outside looking in. With the exception of Aunt Pat, nobody else worked in our house.

The projects were alright for me because I had already, at my young age, learned a lot about living. This was the life, no expectations, no rules, no whooping's, just straight living. The streets were hot, the boys were hot... and the happenings were even hotter. The happenings were everywhere; music loud, hustlers loud, everything just seemed to be so loud. I guess that I should add here that I was the new kid on the block... and I was hot.

The natives wanted to call my country. I put a stop to that real quick because I was a native too. I had just been misplaced for a while, right Brooklyn?

This was home for me now, and I wanted to fit in with everything and everybody. I had a lot of experience with fitting in. Did you get a cigarette? Yeah, I'll try it.

Did you get reefer? Yeah, I'll try it. It went down just like that. I looked for the tough crowd so that I could pretend that I was just as tough. Looking back, I was really just looking for protection because fear has always played a huge part in my life.

I found the cutest, most no-good boy that I could find, and man was he fine, in my eyes. He was tall, slender, light skin and had one of the roundest afros that I had ever seen. He was a good dancer, real smooth like. He made me look good while dancing with him. He was a smooth talker. I remember when Aunt Pat caught me talking to him. She said, *"Stay away from that boy, 'cause he's up to no good!"* What did she know? I was all of thirteen, surely I knew best! Didn't she know that I was almost grown and I had some experience under my belt? Hell, I had even been pregnant once. Surely by now, I knew what I was doing!

How was I to know that he called himself a pimp? He had what he called a stable and wanted me to be his main girl? Well, at least he wanted me to be the main girl! Whew! Thank you, God, for blocking that bullet. That same fine, young pimp was one of the first in the community to die of AIDS? Isn't there a song that goes, *"God Blocked It"*? Yes, I am standing here to testify. I am the evidence.

Record shops/reefer shops where my crew would go to hang out, dance and smoke weed. I remember, oh so well, the nickel bags. But for young girls like me, they had the 'trey bags'. They only cost three dollars. I earned the nickname, 'Tray Bags' because if I couldn't do anything else I could hustle for three dollars for a trey.

I arrived in Brooklyn this time in the middle of the summer when Boz Scaggs was hot. We were really doing it in the park, doing it after dark, in Farragut Park. Man, these were good times. Not better than the 'good ole days', these were just good times.

I had a family! That's really all that I've ever wanted, to belong somewhere. I had a grandmother that lived in the Projects down the block. I was living with Aunt Pat and my cousins on the other block, where the happenings were. I felt as though I had a real family now, and this is where I belonged.

I loved the summertime in the Projects because everywhere we went there were boys… and reefer. I especially liked the 'Rastas', 'Knotty Dread Mon', just my type. They were renegades, just like me.

I would always gravitate to the self-proclaimed underdog type because somehow I had misconstrued the real meaning of the underdog. I gravitated to the underdog because I thought that they were in the struggle like me. I felt as though we needed each other because we understood our struggles. I've always looked for someone to rescue me. Somewhere in my mind, I had this underdog fantasy that if I would rescue you now, that you would somehow, one day gain your strength and you would then rescue me. I needed someone, something to rescue me because I never, ever felt good enough. I would always depend on someone else to make me better. Never did quite work out that way. It's too bad that I didn't know God back then. Had I known God, I could have stopped wasting my time. I was a thirteen-year-old little girl that thought that I had experienced life. That is the story of most thirteen-year-old girls from the Projects.

These were good times and then summer ended. I was taken to Huddle Jr. High School. School? I was too old and too grown to have to attend anyone's school and be in the eighth grade. Did they not understand that I had too many notches of adulthood under my belt for me to be considering school? Well, I guess somewhere there had been a law written about teenagers attending school and if not the guardian would be responsible. That was enough for my aunt to force my butt right down there to 'Huddle Jr. High School'.

I was afraid. I realize that most of my life that I've acted as though I haven't been afraid of anything, but I've always been afraid of everything. Going to Huddle Jr. High School was no exception. I was afraid. Old fears had resurfaced; that gnawing inside, that reminded me that I wasn't good enough.

You remember the man that taught me that when he wouldn't give me the dollar? Those old feelings that had never left just simply, resurfaced for a time such as this. I didn't want to do this. I had no interest in school. I thought that I had enough information for the rest of my life. Why couldn't I go back to the fun in the park? I wanted the music and the weed, not the newness of school. I wanted the 'Rasta Mon,' not Huddle. Okay, let me put my thinking cap on. What was a girl to do?

It wasn't long before I learned how best to deal with this school situation… I got high. Well, they called it High school… didn't they? And that is exactly what I did, I got high! I got high in the morning on my way to school; on lunch breaks, between classes, whenever, I simply got high. Matter of fact, I started selling joints for a dollar to support my habit. We all got high for a while until someone stole my dope. I almost had to fight. I cussed, fussed, kicked, and screamed. I didn't really want to fight because I was afraid. But one thing was for sure, I wouldn't be going back to Huddle Jr. High School… ever.

Actually, as it turned out, I missed 173 days of the eighth grade. When my Aunt Pat finally found out, it didn't go very well. Nope, not well at all. Actually, that was the straw that broke the camel's back; and, in my case, got me shipped back to the south. My poor aunt had tried everything. She had gotten me a mentor, a woman that would talk to me and give me things that my aunt thought may have been missing in my life. The mentor bought me things such as toothpaste, deodorant, hairbrush, and combs for my hair. My aunt was right, technically. These things had been missing... but I had already stolen the things that I needed, so I was good.

This mentor was a friend of the family. Actually, she was a lesbian that was in love with my aunt. She would do anything to get closer to her; even if it meant talking to this little bad ass girl and paying her to act right. I remember this lady buying me books to read. They were actually good books; most of them were on the streets. I had pretty much decided that I would live a life of the streets, but God. I used to hear them say, *"...yeah, she got her mother in her, she can't help it."* Honestly, I could help it. All I ever wanted was for someone to see me, notice me or just tell me that I mattered. If I did matter to them, I wanted them to say so. Lord knows I needed something tangible, something that I could hold on too. I wish that I had known God back then. I began to read the books that my mentor would bring. She would also bring me books that highlighted and focused on the American Muslim lifestyle and teachings. It was my first introduction to God; someone to talk to, something greater than the Projects to believe in. She would bring me books about hoes, pimps, blood, and money. All of the books caught my attention. I was happy that someone could finally see me, I wasn't invisible anymore.

The lady that birthed me happened to have been in

jail at the time and she even started writing me poetry and letters in an attempt to soothe my troubled soul. My soul wasn't ready to be soothed. I just wasn't interested.

Now mind you, even though I had missed 173 days from Jr. 'High' school I became educated in other ways. Believe me, it wasn't easy finding 173 places to go for each of the days that I missed school. I had my adventures. Some of them I will never tell… not even now.

I had friends, and I am not sure, but they may have missed as many days as me. We were always together. Every morning we would meet up at the first building in Farragut Projects. My friend, Gay Gay always had the plan of where we would go for that day.

Some days we would meet up with guys, and on other days we would simply ride the train from one borough to the next, looking for the next thing to do. We would come home at our regularly scheduled time and just meet up the next day to start all over again. Funny, no one ever asked to check my homework, or even asked me what I had learned in school for an entire 173 days. It's not their fault though. I suppose had someone asked I would have given them the most intelligent answer that I could muster up. Well, as usual, every good thing comes to an end and my Aunt Pat found out. I still remember the red, plastic, see-through, jelly belt that she whipped me with. Truth be told, I could have taken all of Aunt Pat's whooping's because I felt nothing. She may have needed to take lessons from my father... now he knew how to whoop! Needless to say that I got forwarded, yep, my butt was forwarded back to the south. Why, why, why!

N. Cack-a-lac

So I am back in North Cackalac, as I referred to this place. Some may call it Charlotte, NC; but it's N. Cack-a-lac to me. I didn't want to be here. I didn't want what this place had to offer me. I was back at my father's house, and he wasn't playing nice. Somehow, he had heard all of the stories of my adventures in the Boogie Down; and for reasons unbeknownst to me, he was not pleased. Okay, for real, I get it now; but I didn't back then.

This was like starting over again. My dad didn't play fair. I told you I was almost grown. But he didn't respect my fourteen-year-old 'grown-ness' at all. He just didn't think that it was cute and there was no compromising. There was no 'having it your way'. There was only one option. 'Do as I say, or get your neck broke'... unapologetically, point blank period!

Being from the Farragut Projects now; and having to appear tough, I pushed every button that I could... even when I knew that the results were going to hurt. Daddy and I got back together and we didn't even have a honeymoon period. He skipped right over the honeymoon and got directly into my behind. I think that he had heard too much and felt as though he had no time to waste getting me back on the right track.

Well, it wasn't easy and it was years before I got on

the right track because I just knew too much. I should have been much smarter than the folks in the Cack-a-lac. I should have been much smarter than my old man. Do all fourteen-year-old girls think like that? Or just the ones that have brown bags, Mason jars, a pregnancy, the Brickyard, and the Projects under their belt?

I had to go back to Jr. High School... dang, it. But that was okay because I still had tricks up my sleeve. Being that I had missed 173 days of school, I was going to have to repeat the eighth grade. We didn't have the internet or fax machines back then, only snail mail. There were no quick ways to look up or retrieve school records. So when they asked me what grade I was in, what do you think I said? Yes, you guessed it. *"I am in the 9th grade"*. Eventually, the principal found out and he came to my class with a plan. He needed a plan because I was in the 9th grade turning it out! But, I showed up every day. I completed more work than I ever had. I was really trying to the best of my ability; I was stilling raising hell though. The principal said to me, *"I have your records and I know that you supposed to be in the eighth grade because you didn't satisfy the curriculum last year"*. He then offered me a deal; because I loved deals, I accepted. I promised that if he would allow me to stay in the 9th grade that I would straighten up and fly right. I guess I didn't know how to fly or straighten up. But he never did put me back in the eighth grade, and I never kept my promise.

One of my father's favorite stories is the one when he was called up to school because I had been extra special this day. He was going to whoop my butt from the schoolhouse to the car... so he thought. If my father was thinking that he was going to whoop me in the middle of the schoolyard, where all of my cohorts hung out, he had another thought coming. Did I ever tell you that I ran a mean 100-yard dash? Oh, well that's exactly what I did. When he pulled that belt off on me, it was a no-brainer! That school had a bridge that went over the top of a highway and I swear I outran several of the cars that were traveling in my same direction.

He didn't catch me that time. But while I was living in the Cack-a-lac, I provided him with many more opportunities. He even learned something else about dealing with me. Never, ever allow me to get a head start. If I couldn't do anything else, I could run.

Chaos

It seems as though I've spent chapter after chapter unraveling the details of my life. I told you in the beginning that this was my story, so I don't apologize. I was at a crossroad, and like all crossroads, I had to choose the best road for me. I chose the wrong road, but hindsight is 20/20. Life sometimes provides us with choices and oftentimes none of those choices are good options. I felt as though I had to choose the least of a lot of evils. I had to make some choices when none of the options were favorable.

For a very long time, I chose death because life didn't seem worth living. It was a mistake for me to think that my past experiences were the best example of what life had to offer. I didn't know that I just didn't know, but I thought that I knew everything.

I heard once that life is about making choices. I was choosing between two dead ends, so I made a choice and hoped for the best. I wish that I had known God back then.

I was able to break some world-class records. I ran a 100-yard dash for 15 years. I was always running; running from my father, running from the dope, running from the thoughts in my own mind, running from fear, running from school, running from pregnancy. Yes, there were many more pregnancies that followed. I was running from the abortion clinics. I ran from the babies that were never born. I was running from the brown bags, running from the Mason jars and running from the Brickyard. I was running from the projects. I ran from the vision of my Mama lying dead in that bathtub. I ran to and then ran from Brooklyn. I ran from that man that told me that 'I wasn't worth the dollar'. I ran until I realized that I was only running in place because I couldn't escape my mind.

I suffer from blank periods of time in my mind. I'm reminded of that age-old joke of what came first, the chicken or the egg, really… which came first? I've pondered in my mind, over and over again, the order of events in my life. I look at my scars and try to guess their age.

I remember being the youngest prostitute in a whore house. I remember being in that house in a room with a trick that kept accusing me of being a boy. He was trying to get his knife out, but he couldn't. He was trying to open the knife up, but it wouldn't. He was trying to swing that blade at me, but he couldn't. I remember in that same house another trick that had his gun and he was determined to kill me, for reasons unbeknownst to me. He was high and had convinced himself that I was the enemy. I am sure that it was all in his mind because I wasn't the enemy. I was just a fourteen-year-old prostitute that had run away from home and couldn't find her way back. He wanted me to do the impossible, as the drugs had convinced him that he was capable of doing what should have been possible.

I remember being frozen in fear as I looked down the barrel of his gun. Somehow through my fear, I managed to scream and call out. I know at this point you probably think that I called out to God. No, I wasn't smart enough. I wish that I had known God back then, but I'm glad that God knew me because none of what could have happened in those days happened. Isn't there a song that says, *"...God blocked it"?* Yes God blocked a lot of things for me back then, but I just became smart enough to realize that it was God that never let me go.

Where I ended up was not where I stayed, but I thought at the time that it would be better.

Fostered Systems

Window Pains, A Testimony of Healing describes the many cracks and streaks of brokenness that I've experienced throughout my life. With all of the chaos that was spinning in my head while I was writing this book, I wondered, 'when would I ever get to the healing? I've come to realize that I've been healing all along. I haven't arrived yet, so keep reading. I've come to the conclusion that the mere fact that I am telling this story is a testimony in itself. I won't downplay that.

This chapter is not intended to place blame on the 'Foster Care System' or any other system that has been designed to replace a natural family existence. 'Fostered Systems' only exist when the natural family cannot, has not, will not or maybe doesn't know how to exist independently and on its own.

Foster systems are a natural consequence and the result of the aftermath of brown bags, Mason jars, brickyards, drug addiction, abuse, poverty, and neglect.

No one realized that generational curses were looming and that these curses would have a hold on our family from that day to this one. I understand now that my arrival into the foster systems occurred long before I ever arrived. It was like destiny. Everything that I had ever experienced led up to the day that I landed in foster care. How was I to know that my landing in the foster system would affect three generations? The cards were still being dealt, but it seemed as though they were never dealt in my favor.

I began this project saying that I would be transparent and I am committed to that. Fostered Systems has been the hardest for me to pen because I couldn't find rhyme or reason here. I am stuck because of the anger that I still harbor as a result of the system, but this is my testimony of healing. My anger doesn't derive from my placement into the foster care system. I survived it. I know that I gave as much as I got. I wasn't easy to deal with. I had already lived through too much. I had seen too much. I had only landed in the system because I didn't want to be hit anymore.

I didn't realize that I would begin a leg of the generational curse that would last for what seemed to be a lifetime. The day that I made that phone call to 911, I didn't know that I would one day have a daughter that would end up in that same system. She ended up in that system running away from a life filled with sexual abuse by grown-ups that were supposed to protect her… because her mother sure couldn't and her father didn't know how.

My daughter and I had more in common with the foster system than we realized. Neither of us got there because we were bad, but it was our experiences as victims that would lead to us both becoming the perpetrators.

On the day that I contacted 911, I had made a decision that would change the course of my life. I remember the call as if it were yesterday. I dialed 911 and waited for the operator. I told her that I had to leave. I remember telling that operator that I was afraid, and I was. I told her that I had been beaten, and I had. I also told her that I would probably be beaten again when my father got home.

I had gotten in trouble, and back then it seemed as though I was always getting into trouble. I had long developed the attitude that there wasn't just very much that I cared about. I spent a lot of days being angry, but there was one thing that I would do and do a lot of; that was open myself up to sexual escapades. I know that some people would say that, 'I was looking for love'. I don't know what I was looking for and I wasn't fooled to think that the boys that I was having sex with loved me. The problem was that I didn't love me. In my effort to feel something, I used sex as a vehicle to feel. I had been pregnant a few times, and out of all of the pregnancies, there was only one girl child born. During the process of healing, I had to eventually let go of the guilt that I lived with because of all of the abortions that I had. Sometimes I wonder who those children could have been, but I guess that I will never know.

I had gotten caught with a boy in my father's house and I was in serious trouble. My father used the best tools that he knew how and I got my butt tore up, beat up punched up, and kicked up. I thought that I was going to die because I had never seen my father that mad. I thought that the beating would never stop, but it eventually did. I tried to get in the bed and I remember my father saying, no! You get on the floor because you are not good enough to sleep in a bed!

The next day when my dad went to work I had put my plan into action. I was getting out of that house, and I thought that I would never come back. I was on that phone calling New York, trying to catch up with relatives that I hadn't seen in years, and my birth mother was one of them. Back then there wasn't any two way or cell phones, it was just home phones, and I wasn't supposed to be on it. I recall my dad's girlfriend trying to get through to me on the phone, but she couldn't because I was trying to call my way out of town. The last thing that his girlfriend said to me was that she was going to tell my father that I was on the phone and that he was going to beat me again, sorry lady, not going to happen!

By no means am I attempting to make my father into a villain here? I know that he had to have been tired and at his wits end. My father uses to tell me, *"Too bad you didn't come with a manual because if you had I would know what to do with you"*. I know now that he was doing everything that he knew how, but he had never raised a girl before. For that matter, I don't think that he ever had to raise anything before, but he did have a dog once.

I found out something about my father much later through family history. I learned that my father had also known about the beatings that Mama used to get from Papa in the *'Good Ole Days'*. I learned that my father had even received his own set of beatings from Papa when he was just a boy, and especially when he tried to help mama. I wonder was this how abuse became another generational scar for our family? Pain perpetuates itself and the cycle of abuse can never be broken if it is never recognized, so let the healing begin.

On the day that I called for help, I had decided that I wasn't going to be beaten again. In my overly dramatic way of thinking, I truly thought that my father was going to kill me with what he labeled discipline… so I called 911. I remember the operator's response to my story. She asked, *"little girl, can I help you?"* I remember saying to her that I wanted to go live with my mother because my father was going to kill me. The operator said, *"well, where does your mother live?"* she had me there because I had no clue where my mother lived. Actually, this had been the first time since I was a very little girl that I even considered the idea of living with my mother. I'm still not sure if that was what I really wanted. I knew that I wanted to be free from my father's house and that was for sure. The operator's response was that she couldn't send a policeman to my house, but if I could get out and meet the officer at this particular location that he would take me to a safe place.

I ran about 2 miles, in my 100-yard dash stride, to get to that location. Maybe I was being overly dramatic, but I knew in my mind that if my father would have hit me again that I was going to die. Many may think, at this juncture, that I deserved all that I had gotten, and you may even be right. But I had to make a decision of how much more I could take. So I ran, I ran far, and I ran fast.

The extent of my injuries was pretty bad. I will never forget the policeman's shock and response to my bruises. *"My Godchild, who did that to you,"* He asked.

I spent the next several years in and out of group homes and foster homes. I was around fifteen years old and my life was already a mess.

System Flaws

The word 'Foster' implies, encourage, promote, stimulate, advance forward, cultivate, nurture, strengthen and enrich the lives of others. The word 'Foster' further implies bringing up a child that is not one's own, taking care of, looking after, and possibly providing for. I never looked at the 'Foster care' system in that light. In my mind 'Foster Care' would mean something not real, not wanted, made up, didn't belong, a substitute for, a poor example of and pseudo safety measures.

The term 'Foster child' meant all of the above and it was the exact equivalent of a misfit. One thing was for sure and two things were for certain and that was I knew the role of a misfit. I had been one all of my life.

The foster system was designed as a measure of protection for children to be kept safe. I wonder though, had I known the full measure of what I would experience in foster care, would I ever have made the call that eventually led me to the system?

Social workers, lawyers, courts, and judges became a part of my life for the next three years. Once, when I ran away, I was tracked down with dogs, there were policeman and sheriffs with handcuffs. There was, at least what seemed to be, one hundred police cars. I quickly became the bad guy in this system I had become a fugitive, but I am certain that they were trying to help... right?

A system is dangerous when it becomes blind to the possibilities of systemic flaws. I was rarely protected by this system, but I guess they did their best.

My experiences were nothing that I had not become accustomed to by now... such as having sex with grown men. My first foster parent worked nights and she needed help watching us while she was away. She had two male friends that owned the club next door that later became known as the 'curve'. She must have really trusted them because she found it not robbery to leave us in their care at night, most nights, almost every night. My foster mother had three of us misfit girls in her home, and one had Cerebral Palsy and talked funny. She would also have seizures and her seizures scared me because I would always think that she was going to die when she had a seizure. Our foster parent was a very nice lady and I actually liked her. I think that she liked us to, but she didn't like us enough to ensure that we were protected.

We weren't allowed to go to that club at night time while the partying was going on; however, they were allowed to come to our house when the party was over. They used to tell me and the other girl how much they loved us. They would easily slip our underwear down to the floor while easing on top of us with the promise of going to the restaurant on the next day. Sometimes they would even give us money, not much money, but some.   Sometimes they would request that we come over to the club in the daytime. They would tell our foster mother that they would pay us to clean up the club. She would allow us to go, and she never came over to see what we were really doing in that club. Cleaning the club had nothing to do with what we were doing with these grown men. We were having sex with them. We really thought that they were our boyfriends. These men were our boyfriends, but we were their secrets… and secrets are never to be told. I don't remember how these relationships began, but I don't even think that it took much convincing on their part to get us to participate. These men were just asking us to do what we both were already accustomed to doing.

    I didn't know that I was being abused because at that time I had so much adulthood under my belt I felt as though I was a willing participant. There is something to be said about grown men that choose to have sex with underage girls or boys for that matter. A pedophile is still a pedophile… even if the child says yes. Children are in need of guidance. Adults should be placed in their lives to lead them, teach them and to help them grow. Never at any time was it acceptable for an adult to have sex with a child, not then and not now, never.

    My foster sister and I would have sex with these men for the promise of a burger and French fries from the new hamburger joint that had just arrived in town.

We weren't having sex for money, although they would occasionally give us money. We would have sex for the promise of a hamburger and French fries. I always got the triple burger.

Eventually, we were found out and our foster mother was angry with the men, and we were moved. I wonder what she told the social worker because no one ever asked me what happened.

I was moved from that house and moved into a foster home, and then I was moved into a group home, and then another foster home. I moved so much that I no longer looked at this system as the foster care system. I looked at it as if it were a moving company that would pack you up and moves you almost like two men and a truck. Does this system is still moving children as fast today? I guess that someone has to look out for the kids, right?

I began running away and that is when the system would use their dogs, policeman to track me, and then handcuffs when they caught me. I wonder if they still use that technique.

Once I was taken to a home out of Charlotte city limits. This was to serve as a deterrent, to prevent me from running away. It didn't work out too well because they were still sending me to Charlotte schools, and I knew my way around. So I ran.

Once I heard that if you ever wanted to get

released from foster care that all you had to do was become pregnant and they would surely let you go. Well, if I didn't know anything else, I knew how to become pregnant. So I put my plan into motion.

First, I picked out the boy. He had to be handsome because I was planning on keeping this baby because I needed it. I met a boy that fits the cuteness requirement and he was chosen. I chose the boy that drove my school bus because, to me, he was fine. It turned out that he lived in an apartment that I could disappear in. It had to be at least thirty-five other people living in that two bedroom apartment. I think they called it a gambling house, but they sold a lot of liquor in that house, and I was used to that. No one cared that I and that young man stayed in the bedroom all day and almost every day. No one asked me where I had come from or why I was there. No one knew, but him that I was a runaway and he hid me out for his pleasure and mine. He didn't know that I needed the baby, and even to this day, I think that he still thinks that my pregnancy was an accident. Actually, it was a planned pregnancy, yes, pregnancy with a purpose.

He would later have to turn me in, and that's when the dogs, the sheriffs, the policemen and handcuffs came. I never forgave him for that until now.

I was taken to live with this lady in Davidson that was a police officer. She had two daughters and on the first appearance, everything looked great, but in actuality, I turned into a real live Cinderella scenario. That woman and her two daughters were wicked and I... was the foster child. The beatings were regular and often. I fought them daily; all three of them until I finally surrendered and ran like I do, 100 yards dash style.

I ran, but this time I was not alone because I found out later that I was with child. True to light once my social worker found out that I was pregnant it wasn't long after that I was worked back into my father's house.

I didn't go into the system because I was a menace, I wasn't the perpetrator; however, I realize that I played a major part in the things that happened to me. In this particular instance, I just needed help, shelter, and protection and I actually received it in that order.

It's Funny how the foster care system works. This system can turn the victim into the perpetrator in the blink of the eye. I thought that the foster care system would protect me, guide me and possibly even nurture my growth, but it never did.

Once a child lands in the system for whatever reason that child doesn't cease needing nurture, but the system doesn't allow for nurture. The system only allows for placement and that doesn't require a heart. It just requires a fire extinguisher, a posted escape route, and it also comes with a warning, *"don't get too attached because this isn't permanent"*.

I did get out of this system and I did go back to live in my father's house, but it was different this time. I was hit one last time by him and then it was decided that hitting wouldn't happen again. I was pregnant and there was a baby that was really going to be born this time. I take my hat off to my father and now he is my hero. He didn't know how to teach me how to be a woman no more than I knew how to be one.

At some point, our relationship changed and it just seemed to work, and my baby was born! Yes, my baby was born.

To my Daughter...

I knew that there had to be something special about you because out of all of my pregnancies you were birthed into creation. I thought that you were created as a means to an end for me, but I know better now. I never had that kind of power, but God did and still does and through his intervention you made it. You see when I enacted my will abortions happened, but when God had just about enough of me, you were born. Your birth was bigger than my plan. You ever hear the joke about making God laugh? It simply says if you want to make God laugh then make plans.

My desire to be rid of a place, a situation, and circumstance led to your birth. I had planned in my mind an escape route, but instead of an escape route, you were born. Beautiful, and full of life, you were my joy, and I loved you with all that I had inside of me. The problem was that I had very little inside I was broken, and scared.

I will never use my brokenness as an excuse for not being your mother, but I just didn't know how to be a mother. I didn't know how to nurture, and love had always been so temporary.

When you were born I couldn't stop looking at you because you were so beautiful. You were smart and very eager for just a couple of weeks old you were lifting your head to check out your surroundings. My father had purchased you a beautiful crib, and blankets, even though he was determined not to like you. He was still angry with me, but he couldn't help but like you because we all basked in your beauty.

My father took you to have your first pictures made when you turned 1 year old. He didn't take me with him because it was his and your time. I still remember the blue and white outfit that you wore that day. I bet that you didn't know that when you were born that you already had a tooth. The doctor said, yes, she is going to be a fast one, and you were.

You began running at 8 months, notice I didn't say walking because you didn't walk, but your first steps were a trot. I am reminiscing because I don't think that you remember your beginnings. You were my baby, and

I loved you as much as I knew how to love, and I am sorry for everything that happened next.

You have grown to be a phenomenal woman through all of your trials, and you had many. I am often amazed to see your face or hear your voice because a lesser woman couldn't have survived.

Your journey would become the same as mine because I provided you with the same experiences that I had. You endured more than I did. Even though you may sometimes stand crooked, you have landed on your feet. You were hurt by those that should have taken care of you. You were hurt by me because I left you, alone, scared. 'If I could turn back the hands of time'... I won't tell your story because your story is yours to tell. Just like your personal healing, baby. You are responsible for your healing now.

I will be forever sorry for your hurts and I wished every day that I could have been a better mother to you. The only way that I survived my epic failure as a mother was by allowing me to get off the hook, and forgiving me as I know that God does. You will have to do the same thing with your children one day. Give yourself a break, let yourself off the hook and accept what was.

I, like you, was a very young mother and I knew absolutely nothing about being your mother. You needed a mother, every child does. I still remember when I needed a mother too.

We've traveled some of the same rounds with a few twist and turns. We both experienced the same systems and its flaws. I, your mother, was in fostered care. You, my child, was in fostered care. And then the babies, your children, were in fostered care. Together we perpetuated a legacy of generational fostered care, but we didn't just create this curse alone. This was learned behavior and we learned our lessons well because we were excellent students.

I thought that I would talk about that next generation of foster children that belong to both you and me. But I will yield the floor to you, my daughter. I can't wait until you are able to release and find your own healing. You may not write it in a book as you may never be ready for the world to know you on such an intimate level. What I do know is that you are going to have to tell somebody, because in order to go to your next levels you will need a testimony of your own healing.

I love you, my daughter. You are a phenomenal woman.

I want to leave you and your offspring with these words of love and encouragement:

To my dear grandchildren....

Babies, the panes represent your squares. Squares that

were prepared especially for you by our Creator... a loving and most merciful Creator. The panes represent you, standing alone, but not being by yourself. The panes represent all of our struggles to come together. Together, we become that beacon in which light shines through.

You see children, each pane, each square with all of the intricacies and uniqueness represents our right to be here. It doesn't matter that often times it felt as though we were standing on the road alone. I bet you may have thought many times that the road seemed like an endless journey. Jacari even thought that the road was hard. Hard never equated impossible, but it did represent possibilities.

Whatever the road means to you, my babies, remember; that through your uncertainties, and amongst all the unfamiliarity, to keep traveling. Remember to change lanes when you must, cross the street when you need to. And please bypass some streets altogether. Please know that in order to reach your pane, your square, your place... you will have to move to reach your destination.

By continuing to move, you will one day reach your designed destination. This will allow you to look out of your pane through the windows of your heart. Then you will be blessed with a freedom that your Creator will work through. Your Creator will begin to heal the many cracks in your panes, the seen and the unseen. Each individual pane will one day be just a glass window with many expressions of Love, with no more regret or self-doubt.

Allow your panes to be pieced back together. I know that you, like glass window panes, have been damaged. You might find that some panes have some cracks; tiny hairline fractures, small holes, and some panes may even be shattered. But whatever state the panes are in, trust me, they can be repaired. A window pane is just one small, framed piece of glass from an entire window. And because one pane is faulty, my own experience has been that the other pieces of the window can hold that broken pane together until the glass repairman, God, arrives. What you have to know and believe is that the pane is repairable.

I hope that whoever picks up this book will be able to relate to the ups and downs of life's struggles. But that's not all that life has to offer. You see, through all of the bad and broken panes we learn to find our own healing. We learn to look at the old broken panes of our lives through new windows of opportunity.

Yes, I know in many instances the damage has already been done, the cracks may seem as though they are unrepairable; however, thinking about window panes, I realize that panes can be replaced with new, creative, transparent glass.

My mother "Regina Lily".

Street Life

So Father, let me get this straight you are giving me a choice of whether or not to stay in Charlotte, with you, and all of these rules... or, I can go back to Brooklyn where there are no rules? I don't mean any harm, but the decision is easy... it's a no-brainer. What time does the next bus leave for Brooklyn?

There used to be a time that if you gave me a choice between life and death that I would choose death every time. Death is exactly what I chose the day that I made the decision to leave my father's house. After all of the running away, sneaking out and hiding from my father, he has presented me with an option; to simply leave. No bells, no whistles, and no fanfare; simply make a decision.

I was waiting for the shoe to drop. Surely he wasn't going to let me leave? After all of the struggles that my father had been through to try and keep me; he was letting me go. I never asked my father why he was letting me go. I wonder... why? Had he felt as though he had failed me? Did he think that I could have done better elsewhere? Or was he just tired of trying to teach a girl how to be a woman? One day I may ask him, but for now, I'm off to my future and I never even saw the destruction coming.

Brooklyn, I don't think that you could ever get rid of me. I am home again, but this time I am better than ever. I have a baby now, surely I am grown now. Surely I can hit the streets when I want to now, surely I can, right Brooklyn?

I'm legitimate, sixteen going on seventeen; a baby and in New York. I made it. I was eligible for a welfare check and W.I.C. Finally, I was grown and deserved to be treated with respect.

There were more drugs, more men, and more money. There was a motto in our house, 'you stay out all night long, and you better not come in the next morning empty-handed'. Somebody in the house would babysit on the promise of getting paid upon my return. The payment could be in the form of drugs or money to get drugs. But there better be payment nonetheless.

I was in training now. I was old enough to learn. Lesson number one… there is no time or such thing as 'Love'. You get yours in cash because love doesn't pay the bills!

I began working in bars because I wasn't getting that concept of no love just money. I was falling in love with every man that I met; however, it seemed as though none of them loved me. If I'm not mistaken they understood the concept of my own house rule better than I did. The men that I met was always trying to get something from me, but giving nothing in return.

I was back in touch with the woman that birthed me and I found this to be strange. I thought that I was supposed to feel something, but I felt nothing for her. I tried to because she was the person that birthed me. Truth be told, I resented the hell out of her because I kept thinking of all those times that I had to make up a mother in her absence. I thought of all those days when I used to wish that I had a mother that would comb my hair. I blamed this woman for everything that ever went wrong in my life; most of all I blamed her for not loving me.

My mother was a real hustler though and she tried to show me the ropes a few times. My mother was one of the greatest thieves, and one of the biggest dope fiends that I had ever known. I am not saying this in any form of esteem now, but there was a time when I wanted to be her. She even had a street name for herself, Jean' Natee. She was the best booster in town, and she was definitely the best dressed.

My mother would take me with her sometimes, but she would often hurt my feelings. She would say, *"...you ain't a hustler, 'because you scared! You need to go to school because you ain't me"* My mother had one major rule for me and that was, however, I was to get mine, I couldn't lie on my back to get it. She would say lying on the back is for lazy women. I wanted to be my mother so bad that it seemed as though I could breathe her air. I hated her with all that I had and loved her with all that I didn't have.

I decided that I didn't need her; and not only did I not need her, I didn't need anybody. Thank God, for not letting me go because that was a little crazy.

I got high to cover my failures in the street game. One fact was true and that was, 'I was not my mother'. I didn't have the notoriety that she had. And I wasn't nearly as slick. I found out that I wasn't slick the hard way. You see, in our house, there was nothing but strong women. Our men were either gone or crazy… I mean literally, crazy. I don't know if the women in our family drove them crazy or whether it was genetic, but they were truly certifiable. They were either clinically ill or dope sick. So the women ran the roost and they were leading men by their nose hairs.

I wasn't gifted like the women in our house because I was always trying to fall in love. I was falling in love with men that were only falling into high and providing me with the dope so that I could be just as high. When I think back I wasn't falling in love I was just falling in high too.

I had a gift though. My gift was simply being young. I guess that I was just something to show off. But it kept me supplied with plenty of dope.

I tried everything from skin popping cocaine to taking acid tabs. I snorted cocaine, but I fell in love with the Heroin. It was something about that nod that made me happy. I thought that I had found my niche. Finally, I found where I belonged and that was anywhere that heroin was. What I wouldn't do for a snort. No, I mean literally... I don't think that there was anything that I wouldn't do for just one snort, to feel that lasting nod.

I finally found that one thing that the birth mother and I had in common; we both liked heroin and that is where we bonded. I was wilding out. I remember that baby that I had; the one that helped me to free myself from the foster care system. Notice that I haven't spoken any more about her? Dope has a way of making you forget your entire reason for existing... I had truly forgotten mine.

I remember the shock that I felt when I saw my father and my baby's father pull up in Brooklyn to get my daughter. My aunt didn't even tell me that they were coming. Had I gotten that bad? Yes, I had gotten that bad. I was a dope fiend. All I wanted was the next fix. I didn't understand though. Wasn't everyone else in the house a dope fiend too? Yes, they were and no one had time to care for my baby. We were all chasing after the same things.

Our family profession was that of being barmaids. We were all good at serving liquor. My grandmother would get me a job and she would say, *"...remember to tell them that you are eighteen."* Well, I was close. Yes, once my father took my baby back to North Carolina, it was definitely open season. I was free to live the life of the streets. No more strings weren't bound by anything and responsible for only me. Truth be told, that was all I had ever been responsible for.

Life didn't get easy for me. As a matter of fact, it became a life of desperation. The streets will take you prisoner, and the rules of the streets or subject to change without notice.

My life was a mess and I was a wreck and I hadn't even turned eighteen yet. Ironically, my family would always say to me when they were mad at something that I had done, 'when you get eighteen you can do what you want to do'. I use to wonder, what more would there be for me to do?

Then I saw him, we lived on the first floor and I use to sit in the window every day and just watch. There was one guy that used to live in our building and every day he would leave out the building and walk by my kitchen window at the same time every day.

I don't know if he was watching for me, but I was checking for him every day. I didn't know who he was or what he did, or even if he already had a woman, but I didn't care much because he was fine. He was 6'3", light- skinned, with curly, blond hair. He didn't speak to anyone in the building and he kept to himself. He always had what appeared to be a scowl on his face and his lips were always twisted. Some may have found these traits of his to be warning signs, but not me, I found him to be mysterious, and I've always liked a good mystery.

Something stirred inside of me when I would see this man, but I don't exactly know what was stirring. Now that I'm older, I realize that it was probably God screaming, No! Danger, Danger!, but I didn't know God back then so all warnings signs were ignored and I went charging ahead into the next few years of chaos, abuse, and pain.

"Out of the Frying Pan And into the Fire"

The streets were hot, the dope was plentiful, and I had just come of legal age, not old enough to have *"good"* sense, but too old to allow someone to tell me what or what not to do.

This was a lethal combination. My aunt had said to me often, *"...when you get eighteen you can do what you want to do"*. Really, so let's put this to the test; make a believer out of me. I planned to marry the mysterious man that lived down the hall. By this time he wasn't mysterious anymore. I knew exactly who he was. He was a dope fiend. I knew that he was abusive; but once again, I found myself 'in too deep'. I was scared because he had already told me too many times that I could never leave. My only saving grace was that my aunt, my father, and maybe even my mother at this point would rescue me from my plight. I was eighteen years old and he was thirty-six, the same age as my mother. I had pushed the envelope too far this time. There was no rescue. Nobody protested. Nobody tried to stop it. Nobody bought any wedding presents or even showed up for support. I was on my own for real this time.

I married the man down the hall that just happened

to be fifteen years my senior. We got married exactly 355 days after my eighteenth birthday. I thought, 'how bad could this be?' He provided the dope, daily. He was getting a welfare check and he had his own apartment. I mean... really, his mother said that he was one of the smartest men that had ever gone to Hunter College. His mother was responsible for paying the rent, his check went to her. I didn't realize the significance of having a 'payee' at the time, but I later learned. I hadn't heard the old wives tale: 'if you want to know how a man would treat his woman, watch how he treats his mother'.

His mother was scared to death of him. He would often become angry, violent and explosive. His mother's husband didn't want him to come to their house because of his violent nature. I think that she was glad when we got married. I think that she may have thought that maybe, just maybe I could fix him or least take some pressure off of her. She used to tell me how smart he was and that he wanted to be a lawyer. He had the potential; even though the only thing he was doing when we met was hustling every day and shooting dope in his arm. Maybe once upon a time, he had potential, but now he only had what he had and that wasn't a lot.

When we first met I hadn't seen the needle marks and puncture wounds in his arm. Even if I had, it probably wouldn't have made a difference. I wasn't in love. I was in fear. He helped me to stay high and provided me with plenty of dope, and for that I loved him. I loved him for helping to ease the fear and the pain that I was beginning to live with daily.

I didn't know that I would eventually become his punching bag. I didn't know that he would want to live vicariously through me. He made me get my GED even though I thought that at eighteen going on nineteen that I was too old for school. I got that GED. I got that GED through the beatings, through the dope, through the pain, through whatever, I got that GED. Actually, I was glad to have the opportunity to leave the house every day to go to school. That was the only place that I could go alone. The man I married became my personal bodyguard. I didn't know that I needed one, but his goal was to protect his investment… me.

This marriage was built on tradeoffs from the very beginning. Each of us wanted something from the other. The problem was that nothing from nothing leaves nothing… broken pain. He saw his future in me, and I saw…I don't know what I saw besides a way to get high for free. I just found myself in too deep. I was too scared to leave and even more afraid of staying. So I did nothing besides getting high, go to school, and fight on a regular basis.

The only good thing that occurred as a result of this union was that I was able to get my G.E.D. For the first time in my entire life, I had accomplished something that couldn't be taken back for bad behavior. 'I wonder if God really meant for me to get my education this way.' I know that I was a little hard headed, but really God, really?

People often say that 'God has a sense of humor'. For some reason, I don't see God laughing at this. If I only had known God back then, but I am so glad that God stood and looked at me as one of his own.

Out of all of the struggles that I had experienced up until that point, I hadn't had a relationship with God, but the tide was turning.

Yes, I received my G.E.D. I can still picture the enormous smile on my husband's face when he came storming into the apartment to tell me that I had passed. We celebrated. He gave me as much dope as I could snort. It was my day! He had his fun as well. He went into that bathroom with his cooker, his syringe, a book of matches and a cotton ball. That was the art of shooting dope, you almost needed a kit. We celebrated until I heard the thump in the bathroom and I became afraid. I went into the bathroom where I found him slumped over with the needle hanging out of his arm. I didn't know what to do, so I dialed 911.

Evidentially, that was the wrong thing to do because the police came with the ambulance. They did something to revive him. But later when he was beating me, he accused me of blowing his high. The police had also taken the drugs. He beat me for a long time that night simply because I had blown his high. He must not have known that I had also saved his life because the police said that he had overdosed. I guess that was just a small inconvenience.

We got over that hump, and he was now planning for my enrollment at a two-year college. Life, as I had become accustomed to, was good again. The dope was plentiful and I was getting high every day. Off to college, I went, and I had a new freedom this time. My husband understood the game much better than I did. He knew that he didn't have to watch me as much because now he had taught me submission through fear. I was terrified of him and he knew it. He had begun to use various scare tactics that were most effective at keeping me in line. He bought me some big glasses. I wore my long hair in two braids on the sides of my head. No longer was I the fashion diva that I had been when we met. No longer was I hip, slick and cool. No longer was I allowed to talk to my family that lived right down the hall, and they didn't talk to me either. Life, as I had known it, had definitely changed, and it wasn't for the better.

In spite of my fear, there was one thing that was certain; that was the fact that I could no longer wait for him to get me high. I was hooked. But now he wanted to dole out the dope as he saw fit. Sometimes he would shoot dope in front of me while explaining to me why I couldn't have any. He was a shooter and I snorted my dope (heroin). I think that my habit was bigger because I could snort a lot more than he was able to shoot. I never fell out or overdosed as they called it.

I had to take matters into my own hands because I had a habit that was calling my name. I had met an old man on my way to school one day. We became friends for almost a year. Just about every morning I would stop by his house and he would give me $20.00 so that I could get a bag of heroin. Once I copped the heroin I would go back to his place. Did I say give me $20.00? Excuse me, he didn't give me anything because there was a price... and I paid with my soul.

"No weapon that is formed against thee shall prosper; and every tongue that shall rise against thee in judgment thou shalt condemn. This is the heritage of the servants of the Lord, and their righteousness is of me, saith the Lord."

Isaiah 54: 17

Scars

I woke up thinking that I was lying on my long, beautiful hair. I would loosen my hair at night and brush it down, so it could breathe. When I was really in the streets, before this marriage, my hair was my identity. As a matter of fact, my cousins and I were known for the richness and thickness of our hair. The same hair that Pat had joked about back in the 'good ole days', had become my glory. Yes, Pat said that it was nappy, and I was ugly. Boy how things can change, especially when you put a straightening comb in the mix. With the exception of the straightening comb, my hair was natural and twice as beautiful. It was my God-given grace. And besides my G.E.D, it was all that I had.

I woke that morning thinking that I was lying on my hair. I was lying on my hair; it just was no longer a part of my head. On one side of my head, he had cut my hair off in patches. On the side of me that was exposed to him he tried to destroy any bit of self-esteem that I may have had left. He had gone in for the kill; this was supposed to be the death blow, the one that would take me out… but God. Yes, I was naked, scared, spiritually bankrupt and at an all-time low. Finally, this man had managed to break me, strip me as he watched me crumble. He had cut my hair jaggedly on one side. He wanted to make me ugly. He needed me to understand that I was his possession and there would be no one that could help me.

Retrospectively, I understand now that he wasn't as smart as he thought he was. He didn't know that he didn't have to cut my hair, or hit me to make me stay. I had been so broken on the inside that I didn't think that I deserved much better than what he was dishing out. I had learned to ignore the internal screaming. I had learned that dope would quiet my insides; I could pretend not to feel. Had he left me outside alone, he probably could have done a much better job of destroying me from the inside out.

Even though I didn't know God back then, what I've come to believe now is that God gives all of his children away to protect themselves. We may not always know how to protect ourselves, but God has given us that ability. We just have to tap into it. God allows me to see things. What I know about me is that I process stimuli from the outside in. God will change that in his time. For now, he has provided me with a mirror that allows me to see me on the outside so I will take flight in order to avoid destruction. It takes a whole lot longer to see the emotional scars. Sometimes we can simply be blind to our internal damage.

"Behold, he shall come up like a lion from the swelling of Jordan against the habitation of the strong: but I will suddenly make him run away from her: and who is a chosen man that I may appoint over her? For who is like me? And who will appoint me the time? And who is that shepherd that will stand before me?"

Jeremiah 50:44

Double for Your Trouble

I had to make a dramatic exit because he wasn't going to allow me to leave, nope, not just like that. I had to go. It took all of the courage that I could muster to finally leave him... leave my beloved Brooklyn.

I ran, and I ran as though my life had depended on it, and in my mind it did. This wasn't the first time that I had to run like my life depended on it so I had some experience in taking flight. I don't know how I got back to Charlotte. I remember being on the Greyhound bus with very little money, God made a way even then. I called my mother-in-law before I left. I told her that I wasn't going back and she scolded me. She told me that I wasn't supposed to leave my husband. She said that I should go back. No disrespect, but that wasn't something that I was willing to do.

I made it to Charlotte and of course he tracked me down soon afterwards. He wanted me back! He understood that he had made some mistakes. But I wasn't going back to New York with him, no way, no how. Finally he had to go back to New York after staying in Charlotte for about a week. My daughter's grandmother and I had taken him to Greyhound. As soon as no one was looking he knocked me down to the ground and got on top of me. He was reaching in his pocket, trying to hold me and take his razor out at the same time. I remember his words, 'If I can't have you, no one else is going to want you'. This was truly one of those 'But God' moments. He tried everything that he could to get that paper off of the razor blade so that he could commence to slicing my face, 'But God'.

He was arrested and eventually released, on the premise that once the police placed him on that Greyhound that he would go to New York. He had to promise to never return to Charlotte or to mess with me again. That was the last time I saw him. That was the last time that I ever wanted to see him. Actually, I didn't want to see him then... he just showed up.

I wish that I could say that I had some sort of epiphany after that ordeal, but I didn't. For many years after that my life was filled with addiction, homelessness, misuse and abuse of my body.

I remained addicted to crack for many years. I ran the streets for many years trying to prove to myself that I was the hustler that my mother said that I wasn't. And she was right because I was never a hustler. When my mother told me that I wasn't a hustler, she had also suggested that I try school. Maybe she did see something in me that I couldn't see in myself at the time. Maybe my mother did have some type of maternal instinct or intuition that I never gave her credit for.

Many years later I shared this story with a man that

had become my friend, he said, *"Yes, you were a hustler, because you survived active addiction, and that wasn't easy"*.

I spent many years trying to find where I fit. It was difficult coming from nowhere and trying to fit in somewhere. I spent so many years trying to kill myself, but never had the courage to simply take myself out. I didn't even know that I was trying to kill myself back then. Only as I look back, can I see that my life was wrapped in self-destruction.

I ran from crack house to crack house, man to man, I was always looking for someone that I felt would be able to save me. But really, who could save me from me? Only God, but I hadn't found God yet. Now I know that God always knew where I was and that is why I am here. One of the most disappointing days that I had in the streets was when a man in a crack house saw me smoking just as much crack as he was smoking. He looked at me and asked, *"What are you doing in here? You don't belong in here!"* That had to be the voice of God coming out of the mouth of a fellow crack head. Don't be fooled. God can use anybody.

The years that followed were filled with pain and suffering, but all of it was self-inflicted. I recall a day when I was having one of my 'feeling sorry for myself days'. I called my father and he met me in a park. Only my father can tell the story of how I was so skinny that my back pockets would touch when I walked. I saw the pain in my father's eyes when he said, *"you will be dead by the age of 28, baby you can't keep living like this"*.

My father would try from time to time to take me to his home and let me live with him, but that never worked. I was too far gone. My life had taken a very bad wrong turn. Neither he nor I knew whether or not I would ever get it together. I thought that too many things had gone wrong and that this was my destiny, 'But God'... and only God.

Out of all the abortions that I had, God allowed me to have one daughter. She, unbeknownst to me at the time, was used by God to save my life. My daughter was going through her own anguish and at that time I didn't have any idea of the hell that she was living nightly. I didn't understand why she never wanted to sleep with the lights out. She was struggling with an anguish that would scar her to the core of her soul. I will always pray for her healing.

My daughter's grandmother had a heart to help. She didn't care who you were; if she could help you, she would. She would help, but there would always be a price to pay; nevertheless, she would help you. Her house was always a place that I would be able to return to because I was the mother of her very first grandchild whom she loved dearly. One particular morning I arrived at her house after being in the streets for several days. I was smoked out and in desperate need of a place to rest. I lay on her bed crying as I would always do after the dope had run out. I was crying and feeling sorry for myself as usual. My daughter spoke the words that would eventually save my life. She looked at me crying in that bed. She had such a look of disdain on her face when she said, *"What are you crying for, now?"*

I didn't understand then the significance of what she was saying, but now I do. I know now better than I ever had before the implications of that statement. As I said earlier, her story is her own to tell, and I pray that day will come when she is able to release it to the world and find her own healing.

I wanted my daughter to feel sorry for me, to help me to understand my pain. She was in the 5th grade at that time and for her very short life she had been fending for herself. And now I wanted her to feel sorry for me, and my past. At her very young age she already had a past of her own.

I realize that nothing happens under the sun without our God being aware of it. I do believe that everything happens for a reason. God used my daughter in a mighty way on that morning because I heard her that morning. I heard God loud and clear. I am not so selfish as to think that my daughter's birth was simply to provide the statement that would eventually change my life; however, I am now connected to God in a way that allows me to better to recognize his actions.

I was angry with my daughter when she made that

statement, but the truth often has a stinging affect. What was I crying for? Crying because I couldn't stand my own self, crying because I was responsible for the mess that I had made with my life, crying because there was no longer anyone to blame for my life. I was crying because the pains in my life were like window panes. There were cracks, streaks, broken panes, and discarded shards of glass lying everywhere in that mess that I called a life.

I was angry at my daughter because at that moment that little fifth grader, with the long, beautiful hair, was standing in the mirror trying to prepare her own self to catch her school bus. I was angry because my daughter at that moment reminded me that I had failed terribly. I was angry because at that moment my complaints about my life had become hers; and not only was I in no position to help her plight, I didn't even know half of her story.

My baby that had once been my trophy, because of her beauty had been failed by her mother. My failure was starring me in my face asking me that question, *"What are you crying for, now?"*

Why was I crying? Maybe because the breakthrough was on the way and there was turmoil before the calm.

I was drained; I couldn't run from the horrors of myself any longer. I couldn't hide behind the dope. I was going to either get free or die. The time had simply come for me to make a decision concerning my life. As I think about it, I wasn't making the decision at all. God had put his foot down and the next decisions that were made were truly His.

I had come to Charlotte running from an abusive husband, but I ran right into the abusive streets. It wasn't by accident that I found the streets because I had a habit of looking for my own destruction. I came back with a dope habit that had exploded. I didn't even realize I had a habit until the morning I had woke up dope sick. Crack crippled me, but there was nothing like that heroin habit that I had succumbed to. The withdrawal had to be the worst experience in the world. I remember during withdrawal I had lost the ability to walk for a day. I experienced paralysis for a day or so, but wouldn't go to the doctor.

I needed a fix and I never understood how or when my life had become so dependent on drugs. Drugs had been so easily obtained that I never knew that I had a problem. I had accepted drugs as just a part of my life and I thought that was the way everybody lived.

I even tried my hand at being a drug dealer, but I had to quickly get a job in a fast food restaurant. I sold drugs for about a year or so right there on what use to be Kenny Street. I hung with the best of them. I even dated the robber so that he wouldn't rob me, that was genius right? Well, he told me later that he wouldn't have robbed me because he didn't rob women. It would be crazy for me to think that God only shows up one way because God has showed up in my life in so many ways. All I can say is Thank You God for saving me as I consistently tried to change your plans for me.

I had to turn to selling myself for drugs. But selling me wasn't new because I had been selling myself for a long time. I just have to be transparent about who I was and continue to be thankful that I no longer practice those same behaviors. I did everything on the down low though, because even as a dope fiend I had some pride. It has always mattered to me what people thought about me. For that reason, I know that God has everything to do with this book, and not me.

Anything else that I could add to this story from this point would be repetition and further horrors of my addictive lifestyle. Now, I can tell you that the woman that birthed me was the first person that had ever given me a crack pipe. Her logic was that she wanted me to know what was out there in the street. She knew that I would eventually run into it, and I did. I didn't like it initially when she gave it to me, but I later learned to love it. I could tell you the horrors of two other marriages that came later, but that's not really necessary. I married different faces, different names, but they all were exactly the same. I don't want to sound bitter or even blame the husbands because the common denominator in them all was me.

Yes, I was homeless for many years during my twenty's, but I only had to sleep in the streets a few times, and the shelter once, 'But God'. Actually, I am done with the war stories. I have taken what I can get from those experiences and I have moved on. Those days are gone, but not forgotten and now there is a Testimony of healing.

You see, the morning that my daughter asked me that life changing question of, 'what was I crying for now?' My life changed in a drastic way. I left that house that morning and although I never looked back to the dope, well at least not until fifteen years later, (and only for a short period of time) my life had changed. I was able to stop using drugs, the moment I walked into that room and announced that, *"My name is Tracey, and I am an Alcoholic".* Being an alcoholic was the only thing that I would cop to although; drinking was never something that I had done. I think thanks should go to Johnny Walker, and Mason Jars, for that one. Coupled with the fact that I never did like drunks, contributed to my not being a drunk. Nevertheless, I walked into that room and made the announcement. I was so desperate that it really didn't matter where the help came from. God had used my daughter to wake me up, and snap me out of my stupor. I couldn't turn back.

"I can do all things through Christ which strengthened me."

Philippians 4:13

Clearing the Wreckage

When God used my daughter's voice to ask me that question, *"What are you crying about now?"* That was the first day of the rest of my life. God was moving in a mighty way that day. Through all of my tears, and self-inflicted pains, God was moving. I remember trying to sleep that morning, but I could not. I got up and found a telephone book because I needed somebody to help me. I was as desperate that day as I was on the day that I had called 911, trying to leave my father's house.

I had to leave the place in which I was that morning. The place that I was leaving was not just a physical space, but it was a spiritual place.

I didn't realize that I had been trapped into spiritual bondage. I didn't understand then what God had to do with all of this. I'd never had a relationship with God. God was never a consideration. Actually, I thought that God was never concerned with me and that was just what I thought.

I had gotten baptized at the age of twelve, during one of the times that I lived with my father. I'm telling you, in my 'Father's House!' With the exception of times in my father's house, I never heard about God. I didn't grow up in an environment where God and His grace were discussed. I grew up in homes in which the rule was do as I say, but not as I do. That didn't work though, because I did what they did... on steroids.

I had to leave this place in which I was fighting to keep the men off of me at night. I would have never have imagined that they were also getting at my little girl; I just never thought that would've happened to her. But for what happened to her, I will forever ask that she forgives me for not knowing; for not taking her with me right away. I thought that I would go and make a way. By the time I returned for her she was already bitter, angry and broken.

I was no longer in charge of what was happening because it was obvious that I didn't know how to live. I had long since stopped snorting heroin, and God was cleaning me up from crack; however, it was the wreckage of my past with which I had to deal. No longer could I smoke crack for two or three days, and then cry myself to sleep while lying in the fetal position. God wouldn't allow me to sleep any longer. It was time for me to leave a physical place and to walk into something spiritual, but I still didn't know what to call what was happening to me then.

But I had to get up because it was if God was saying *"Get up and leave this place",* remember what he told Abraham? You will have to go back to the beginning for that one.

I had two bags of clothes, $60.00 in my pocket and nowhere go. But I had to leave the place where I was.

Funny how Satan will always show up when God is on the move (he ain't learned yet!). The first place that I went was to the boarding house down the street where I used to smoke crack. Now, I can hear God saying, 'Really Tracey, Really?'

So let me tell you about this miracle. I paid my fellow crack users the $50.00 for the room, rooms were cheap back then. She gave me the room directly across from the kitchen where everyone was smoking crack. You see that's how I know that God had my back even when I didn't recognize Him. Surely, that was the best that I could come up with, 'But God'. I was in that room and on my knees praying that I wouldn't walk out the room and smoke crack. I was praying like Jesus was prayed in Gethsemane that I wouldn't smoke crack. They were right there in the kitchen smoking. Man, I could hear the sizzle. 'But God'

My fellow crack smoker knocked on the door, and told me that she couldn't rent me the room, and she handed me my money back. I didn't have the strength or the courage to do what happened next. As she was standing there with my money in her hand with that look in her eyes that said I just need one more hit.

I took my money out of her hand and grabbed my bags and left. Now that was God!

Once again, I wish that I could have said that my life had come around full circle, but of course it didn't. I had stopped using drugs, but my life required a spiritual cleansing because it seemed as though my life could have been deemed a disaster area. My life looked like Hurricane Katrina had hit it and I needed all kinds of relief packages.

Talking about being prophetic, my father had once told me that I would die as a direct result of my addiction by the time I turned twenty eight. By the time I turned twenty five years old God had sent me to Alcoholics Anonymous for my first foundation. And by the time I turned twenty eight he had sent me to Narcotics Anonymous. My father had never been more right. I did die, but I had the opportunity to be born again.

The next phase of my life would require a different kind of strength. Actually, it was a replacement of a pane that had been cracked in my window of life.

I was clean and sober for the first time since I was 13 years old. I had a new perspective on my life and God was preparing me. It wasn't long after that I was able to first finish a two year degree, and then my undergraduate degree. It would be several years later before I would receive my next educational achievement. My Masters in Divinity was my greatest achievement, but that was much later while I was in another very different type of storm.

I was three years clean and sober. I was fighting for

my daughter who at this time really didn't want to have anything to do with me. She had already lived through abuse, neglect, group homes and foster homes, and she had no need for me. At the age of thirteen she had made a decision much like the one that I had many years earlier; that was that she no longer needed a mother.

My daughter had run away from home. She had been gone for a while. Out of the blue one day she called me to tell me everything that had ever happened to her. She told me the exact people that had harmed her and she said, *"I'm not going back"*.

As she started re-telling her own horrors I was reminded of the Grace that God has shown me and I was convinced that God would show her that same Grace. Before the conversation was over my baby dropped the bomb. She said, *"I'm pregnant"*. My thirteen year old daughter was living on the street and was about to become a mother.

I remember just listening, crying on the inside. I was wondering, 'what did either she or I know about being someone's mother?' I cried because I could see another generation of lost souls. Although I had a relationship with God, I wasn't sure what he was going to do with this.

She had the baby, a beautiful baby boy. By the time he reached eight months he became my baby boy. I picked him up from the nursery where he was left and kept him until he turned three years old.

Most of my growing up had occurred in these new formative years. It was as though God was providing me with an opportunity to make it right. As I said, these were my new formative years and I was still learning. One thing that I learned was that the past was gone and anything that I received from this point would be new and different. I had to stop trying to make up for what had been done. I had to learn to forgive myself and live this new life for what was being presented in each new day. I couldn't continue to be held hostage by a past that God had freed me from.

My daughter would come and live with me from time to time. She was the one person that reminded me of my failures.

It was not what she said, (well not all the time), but it was her life that was speaking very loudly. I always felt that had I been a better... then she would have been a better... but by His Grace. Every time my daughter showed up, I felt as though God was punishing me. That girl was something to contend with. She was angry, and rightly so.

I still don't have any intentions on telling her story; even though so much of her story is entwined in mine. Forgive me daughter in advance, but our lanes will always cross... I am your mother.

My daughter reminded me once that, yes, I had

found recovery, had new books to read and meetings to attend; but what was there for her? How would she find recovery? I honestly didn't have an answer, but now I know about His Grace. My daughter was a pane from the window of my life that would have to be repaired, 'But God'.

"But be ye doers of the word, and not hearers only, deceiving your own selves."

James1:22

Saved, *but maybe not* Sanctified

I've heard that statement so many times, *"I'm Saved and Sanctified"*. Well, if being saved was just the confession of knowing Jesus, I was finally saved, but I was so far from being sanctified. As a matter of fact, my sanctification continues to happen daily as I repent of every old and new mistake that I make.

Finally, I began to reflect on many of the things that my father had spoken into my life. I remembered when he would say things like, *"you need to get saved and get back into the church"*. I used to think, 'saved from what'; God had already allowed everything that could have happened to me to happen. My life had catapulted. I was well into a second marriage. Although I was clean and sober my husband wasn't and this was an emotional disaster. I stayed in this marriage for twelve years and after twelve years of being clean and sober, it was the devastation of this marriage that sent me into using drugs again.

Ironically, I was older now and determined that this marriage was going to work, even if it killed me... and it almost did. But I hung in there like a trooper; almost like the postman, through rain (addiction), sleet (abuse), and snow (fear). I hung in there. It was the last year of living in that marriage in which my life took a major turn, but not for the better.

I had been married to my second husband for twelve years before it ended. In our twelve years of matrimony, we had moved 12 times; either because I was running from, him with an idea of never returning, or I was following him to try it differently this time. The straw that broke the camel's back was when we had accumulated three of my daughter's (by then) five children out of the foster care system, and fighting for the other two.

We were living in Durham, and I had begun to take the children to this small church that I had found. I had stopped going to NA meetings, and I no longer had my support group. I had lost touch because I couldn't keep up with the man and my spiritual and emotional health at the same time. As always, I chose the man over what I knew to be right. I was saved, but not yet sanctified; however, I was thankful that we were in the Church.

I had these kids in church and I was determined to give them a life that would be different from the life that I or their mother had lived. I was a little late because these children had already experienced more horrors than I could have imagined. The children had come out of a foster placement in which they had been sexually molested over and over again. The acts that were performed on them were the same acts that they would perform on each other later. The system wasn't helpful because they denied that anything had happened on their watch; therefore I was left to deal with the damage to the children's past. I was devastated because once again my own failure continued to show up in the damage of the lives that began a generation before me.

I felt hopeless and it appeared as though this cycle would never end. All hell had broken out in my home. You see, the man that I had taken care of emotionally, for the last 12 years wasn't emotionally stable enough to understand the needs of the children. I was so busy trying to atone for my past that I missing what was happening in front of me.

My focus and time had shifted and I didn't know how to balance my time. The children were tugging on me constantly to meet their needs. My husband and my grandchildren were in a tug of war, trying to get their emotional needs met. He fought with the children often. Because I had lost my child and was determined not to lose these, I fought with him about fighting with them. I had taken a stance and I would protect these kids with all that I had, and with all of whom I was.

There was one thing that I hadn't taken into account, and that was that after all of the years that he had gotten high while we were married; with all of the homes that I had left, and all of the geographical changes that we had made. I had never considered that he would use one last thing to get his wife back.

I had picked up the kids from afterschool care, and I had gotten home a little earlier so that I could prepare dinner. I know that my husband was home because he had a worker's compensation case going on and had been out of work for the last year. I didn't know that after all of the doctor visits and all of the lawyers that he had settled for a check somewhere in the amount of thirty-three thousand dollars. He was celebrating. I walked into the back room of our house and in that room, I had seen something that I hadn't seen in the last fifteen years, and that was a plate of crack. At first, I tried to walk away, but it was calling my name. I couldn't resist, I had no support system, I was saved, but not yet sanctified. I tried with all that I had to walk away, but then he called me back, and he asked this question, *"Can you hit just one?"* And I said yes. Needless to say, that I did the best I could to raise these kids high for the next three years. The kids never knew it because I maintained my job and went to work every day. The relationship with my husband deteriorated quickly. I eventually put him out and took the children back to Charlotte.

I stopped using dope eventually and started attending my home church, St. Paul Missionary Baptist Church. It was where I was first baptized. I had the children involved in children's church. They were baptized and we had become a part of the church community. After several years of stability, I even took my husband back, but he would never attend the church with us. I had started teaching Sunday school, and that had become the highlight of my week. My husband wasn't using, the children were doing better and I thought that life was good, well at least it appeared to be good.

The children were having visits with their mother and I was told that the plan was reunification. Instead of me helping the process I wasn't supportive because I wanted the children to stay with me, I wanted to ensure their success. I am a believer now that everything happens in God's timing. I was fighting on one end and my daughter was fighting on the other. She was fighting for her rights as their mother, and I was fighting for an opportunity that I had missed long ago.

I had to fight the system on a regular basis in support of my grandchildren. I had just fought to keep the youngest from being adopted by some people that I had considered strangers, well I didn't know them. I fought with the Department of Social Services from the bottom to the top, and I got my granddaughter. Again, I thought that life was good and I was now managing four children and a husband. I was in the process of adopting these children as my own. Physically, I was at the heaviest weight that I had ever been in my life. And although I was managing, I wasn't happy. It seemed as though I had to fight to keep this life together.

I was still teaching at Sunday school thanks to a deacon that had seen something in me. My pastor was encouraging me to attend Seminary school, and that was the ridiculous idea that I had ever heard, but he kept after me about this. I had no plans of ever attending Seminary. God and I were good, but um... that was about it for me... saved, but not yet sanctified.

Another life-changing moment...It happened in two days. After fighting with DSS and my daughter about her children for what seemed a daily routine. I found myself always needing to defend my actions with these children. I was unaware of the ongoing investigation concerning me spanking these children. The children were being questioned in school about whether or not they were being spanked. I have to admit that they had received a few. But they only received spankings on the days when I was just regular ole 'Mama', not on my foster parent days. I had become a licensed foster parent by this time because I couldn't afford to support all of these children on my own. If only I could have seen into their future, I would have given the payments back and just kept my grandchildren safe.

The department decided that they would take the children from school and place them in another home because it was alleged that I was spanking them. It didn't matter that the children weren't on medication and were doing better in school than they ever had. It didn't matter that I was ensuring that the children were receiving therapy and other community resources due to sexual abuse that they had received in previous placement prior to them being placed with me. None of that mattered. The plot had been put into action long before I was aware. The children had begun to act differently at home. They had become more defiant, and one of them even said, "The social worker said, you can't touch us!" I knew then that it was the beginning of the end, but I was blindsided by their next move. The Department had taken my grandchildren away. There was a siren that rang out through my entire soul and it cried out failure. The children that I had invested in for the last several years were gone. My white picket fence had been torn down with the ink from a pen, it was gone.

The devastation wasn't completely over, no not yet because it was the very next day that my husband had decided that he was leaving and he wasn't coming back. His long-term girlfriend had decided that he could live with her until he got himself together. I thought he was already together; he was working, not using drugs, and living with his wife… me. Within two days life as I had known it had come to an end, but it was that third day when things began to make sense.

After being in my pajamas for two days; not combing my hair, not bathing, not brushing my teeth or eating, I made a decision. I walked outside to just check the mailbox. I wasn't expecting anything, I was just trying to motivate myself to get up and get out of the bed. God was in my ear, but I was angry. Why God, why do I have to get up, now? You have stripped me of my hope, my future, and now I can't even lay here and waste away! It began to feel as if I was suffocating and I needed air. I got up and went outside to the mailbox just as I was. My hair was standing on my head, I was white around the mouth, and I was angry. The mailbox was located all the way at the end of the driveway, so I slowly and defiantly walked to that mailbox. In that mailbox was an application packet from Hood Theological Institute. I had not requested it, I had not been interested, and I had no desire to attend Seminary before now, 'But God'. A wretch like me!

I looked at that packet and right before I got defiant and threw that packet in the trash can, God placed something on my mind. What else do I have to take from you before you start to hear me? My response was *"...nothing God. You don't have to take nothing else."* I was saved, and now on my way to sanctification, the saving of my soul. I was on my way to learn about God in the way that He wanted me to understand Him. God was breathing into my soul, and he let me live.

My Seminary experience was like being in the midst of God's sense of Humor. First I have to say that I never saw this coming either. I didn't know that my life experiences were preparing me for this moment. How could this be, after all of the mishaps of my life? Seminary?

Once again I found myself in the midst of people

where I felt as though I didn't quite fit. Everyone was so Christian and I was still so Hood, maybe I was in the right place because it was *"Hood Theological Institute"*. I had the best experiences of my life in this place, and I must say that I didn't make straight A's, but I came out it all with a relationship with my God that was better than it had ever been.

I realize that it doesn't take seminary to meet God, but God will always choose the meeting place, and seminary just happened to be mine.

It is through God's Grace and Mercy that I am now an ordained minister with a Master's of Divinity degree. It was only through God's Grace that I was able to sit through a Theological Seminary feeling as though no one had ever gone through the things that I had gone through. Or, Maybe, I was the only that was willing to admit that I had been shattered like the panes in a window. Not all at one time, but in sections, in panes. But now the window of my soul is like the windows in a church, the panes are colorful, vibrant, and they remind me of life.

It is now through this testimony of healing that I live and through the Grace of the Almighty that my panes have become colorful.

Thanks for letting me share.

My father died prior to me finishing this book, and prior to him finishing his own book, "What in the Hell Happened to Me?"

In dedication to my father I have included the pages that he wrote and cherished so much.

I remember when we were on the cruise for my sister's wedding, and he followed me around the entire ship until he finally convinced me to take the time out to read his words. I didn't want stop and take the time out to sit and read his legal pad full of words, but God!!!! I got sea sick for an entire day and I couldn't leave my room and the T.V. didn't work!! The only thing that I had to do was to read his book!!!

I hope that you enjoy the excerpt as it was my father's words.

Thanks

Carl Henry Taylor

What the Hell Happened to Me?

By

Carl Henry Taylor

Introduction

Greetings! I don't know about you but I often look back on my life and say to myself, "What the hell happened to me?" As I headed my life in one direction, I would find myself in a position or location I was not trying to get to, sometimes good and sometimes not so good because of my decision or someone else's or sometimes just circumstances. Yet and still I would say, "What the hell happened to me?" But all in all, those things made me who and what I am today. I pray that something in my book will help you on your journey.

This book has been one of the hardest things I have ever done. I think I should have done it sooner in my life when I didn't have so many memories. But at this late age, I have a ton of memories. Sometimes they come to me a little at a time and at other times like a flood. The thing about memories is sometimes the passage of time will give you clarity and understanding; some memories will always bring joy and oh yes, some will bring sadness. You have to determine how yours work for you.

If we were poor, I could not tell. My grandmother always worked mostly in the tobacco fields and my uncle was retired from the military or something. We never went hungry that I can recall. In tough times my grandma could make chicken feet and rice taste as good as steak, which I can never recall having. It is funny, as I think back on those days how little it took to make one happy. Kool-Aid in penny packs was the highlight of a meal. If mama had extra money, I would skip to the store just giggling "gone have Kool-Aid, Kool-Aid." The smells from supper would fill that house and we were a family, as far as I knew. I can't recall any harsh words or any kind of arguing during these early years. I never asked about a dad for I felt we were complete.

My great-grandmother was awesome. She lived a couple of blocks from us. She was a Cherokee Indian and boy was she strict. When she stopped by on some weekends, she would have us to wash the front porch with lye and hot water and on Wednesdays she would make lye soap in the backyard once a month. I would hang around them trying to understand "Pig Latin" which they would speak when talking about something that was too much for my young ears. Wilson, North Carolina was my world and I loved it; had everything I thought good times were filled with- love, family and adventure.

My next door neighbor Ed and I would make sling shots out of bicycle tires, tubes and show tongues attached with strings and we would become bird hunters. Never got one but boy the fun of the hunt life was great. At times in my life when things and times get rough, I can pull up some of those times and they seem to soften the blows. I remember things are not always bad. This lifestyle lasted about seven years. There were somethings that made sense to me later in life like why did my Uncle Freddie seem to have his friend spend the night on weekends. They would always slink out in the mornings, never saying good morning or good bye, just out the front door. My grandmother never said a word or complained about these guys, yes guys. I later learned my uncle was gay but he was still a great uncle to me and son to his mother.

Life was great but certain parts were kept away from my life. My mother had what I later would find out was her boyfriend. His name was Harvey and the only real memories I have of him was his smooth style and he rode a motorcycle. That was rare in our town. And I recall mother coming back from a ride with Harvey and she had some burns on her thigh. On another occasion, he took us for a ride out into the country, into a corn field and they brought corn whiskey during those years. My mother's personal life was kept down low, there never was a parade of men in and out of our house. My grandmother would not have that out of her but my uncle was a weekend hoe.

His life style would not affect me until my early pre-teen and teen years. Yes, yes, life was great or as good as this seven year old understood. Then it happened, I don't recall any conversation. Just one day my uncle from New York came to town. Yes my Uncle Albert, he was the first hustler I ever met. He dressed sharp with a rolled brim hat and a little brake in the brim. He had a car, yes, a car. It was black as about all cars were in those years due to the recent end of World War II. And Uncle Albert did not even talk like the other men in Wilson. He spoke "proper" English and after about a week, he said we, my mother, sister and me were going to New York to be with my father (who I said to myself) I had no desire to leave this slice of heaven in Wilson and who was this father they were talking about. I did not know him or feel a need for him.

I was not happy on the morning of our departure. I ran upstairs and hid behind what was called a "Shiftrow." It was just a tall clothes closet on wheels. I held on to the top with my feet off the floor so nobody could see my feet. I held on for what seemed like an hour listening to everyone call my name, "Jitterbug, Jitterbug." Boy, you better come on out where ever you are! But, I finally had to let go and I was caught. I cried and cried as I thought of all I would be leaving at my early age. Yes, there was a girl, Jackie Christian, who I would walk to school. It was a little Catholic school on N. Reid

Street. I would tell my mother to tell Mrs. Romain's daughter, a dark-skinned girl, I had already left for school. Then, go get this high yellow sweetie. My mother would do it sometimes and sometimes, she would not since Mrs. Romain was her running buddy. And now I was about to leave all this!

Cry as I might, they tied two chicken coops to the top of my uncle's car along with suit cases and we headed to New York. This was the early fifty's and a change in all I knew. I guess this was the first time I asked, "What the hell happened to me?" This change in my life, which I had no control over, yet here it was, moving to Brooklyn, New York, a place I had never even heard of or cared about. The first major change in my life was one that I look back on with the old "what if thoughts." growing up in a small town and how great I thought that would be, but later life would change those thoughts.

Well anyway the move was on. I never will forget my first thoughts as we got into Brooklyn. First there was no grass, no trees and all the houses were stuck together (all Brownstones). We pulled up to our new house at 332 Macon Street, one room on the ground floor with a shared kitchen and bath. I never will forget seeing my "father" for the first time in bed reading. He did not get up to welcome or help unload our bags. This nigger was cold and it appeared obvious, we were not welcome. This was my first contact with my father. We all lived in this one room and my mother and father slept in a bed in the front of the room. My sister and I shared a small bed against the wall. The only other furniture was a floor model radio. This was our only form of entertainment. I listened to Long Ranger, The Shadow and The Green Lantern. This was the first radio I'd ever listened to. We had a small one in Wilson but it only played on a Sunday morning. There were no night time stations heard in Wilson. So, my life changed from the family life at night in Wilson listening to my grandmother tell us stories or just sitting on the porch in a rocking chair just rocking and listening to the crickets. Yes, it was simple but it was enough and now in Brooklyn, no friends. This was when I started to develop my imagination in my first days in Brooklyn.

I remember on the first Saturday of the week we were there, my mother sent me around the corner to the meat market to get a pound of hog brains for breakfast. So, I went in and asked the butcher for a pound of brains. He thought I was being funny and told me to take my ass back home. New Yorkers didn't know good eatin'. Sometimes, I try to search my mind for some good times on Macon St. but I find none. But my mind does recall the first time my father struck my mother. It was in that shared kitchen. I don't know what he hit her for but I do remember the upstairs neighbors,

Joe and Vera were at the kitchen table. I begged them to make him stop but they did nothing, so I grabbed his pant leg and he back handed me in the face causing my nose to bleed. Nobody had ever struck me like he did. I would like to say it was an accident but it wasn't. That's been over sixty years ago and it's still fresh in my mind. So I would urge any man that does this kind of abuse to know how long memories of these type of actions last. It took me a long time, myself, to understand this and the effects of how your actions, good or bad, affect people in your life but I just can't say maybe not understand but CARE!!!

To say my life was changing is an understatement. New people came into my life; uncles and cousins, folks I never knew or heard of on my "father's" side of the family: Aunt Helen and Uncle Jerome, Cousin Jessie, another grandmother "Mama" and her husband Bernice and it went on and on. Then there were family gatherings at their respective homes and alcohol was always a part of these gatherings. I know on occasion, in Wilson, my mother and her friends would go and get some corn whiskey but never brought it back to my grandmother's house but not this new family group. I can't recall a family gathering that alcohol was not a part of the game and these niggas were not social drinkers and drank to get drunk and the "fun" began every time. Yes, the fight would break out and it would always start the same way. Someone would say where so and so lived in Wilson and then someone would say "you're a god damn lie, they lived somewhere else" and it was on. As a child, I connected the fights with pigs' feet because they always had pigs' feet at these gatherings. Those little pigs' feet bones would be all over the floor after one of these brawls. And to this day, I don't like pigs' feet.

Another strange thing about these family gatherings: A few weeks later, they would meet at another family member's house like nothing ever happened. I'm glad nobody ever really got hurt. They never used any weapons, just drunks brawling. I can laugh now but back then, it scared the hell out of me!

This New York life was a big change from my country hometown life and now I can look back and see how the first building blocks of my life were made and the seeds were planted.

Chapter 2

My Own Room

I don't remember exactly how long we lived on Macon Street in that one room but one day my father announced we were "moving" to the "Projects." I had no idea what a "Project" was but I was glad to be getting out of that one room and I was ready to see and learn new things. The lady on the third floor on Macon St. had invited my sister and myself to come up and watch "TV" which I had never heard of. Boy, was I surprised when we went upstairs to her house and watched the circus on her "radio" that showed pictures…a "TV."

Yes, a whole new world was opening up to this seven year old country boy. The year was about 1957 or so but we were moving to the Farraqut Projects in Brooklyn. It was new and we were getting a brand new apartment. I would have my first "own room" and my own bed. This was great. We moved into 177 Sawd St., Apartment 9D. This building had elevators. My room was not very big but it was "my room." We had our own kitchen and living room. This was great you would think but if attitudes and lifestyles don't change, location makes no difference in your family life. We still had the drunken brawls but now we could have some at our house now because we were out of the one room and into our new home.

But I must be honest, there was some good times in these early years. The games of shooting marbles in front of our building making carpet guns out of wood rubber bands and clothes pins, scotters out of milk boxes, two by four and old skates. And speaking of skates, everybody kept a skate key on a shoe string around their neck. Yes, these simple things kept you happy. Toys we usually made by hand, no X Boxes or other costly things, just your imagination and in the "Projects" was the first time I lived in a place where other races lived. Also, my world was expanding. I saw how other families lived. They seemed to be happy sitting on the benches in front of the buildings during the summer laughing and talking. I can recall my parents sitting out front. My dad never did. Yes, I said dad because by this time, I learned to call him "daddy."

We had molded into a family, not perfect, but a family; not a love and kissy, kissy family and it worked until alcohol was involved. Then we never knew how the day would end if mother held her tongue, no fight would break out. Oh yeah, she would take a drink or two and she would go word for word back with my father. Now, I must confess this was not every week and not often enough that I got used to it but enough that each time, it got me out of my comfort zone and reminded me not to get used to peace and quiet. Some may ask about the good times and what, if anything I learned from my dad. Well, no matter how bad it got, he kept us well fed and a roof over our head, never on welfare and he was a provider. Yeah, sometimes I went to school with a hole in the soles of my shoes but that was rare.

My mother worked too. Believe it or not, she worked in a toilet seat factory and every now and then, she would come home with a toilet seat or two and hook her friends up. I have no idea how she got a toilet seat out of the factory but she did. Yes, even back then you could get a hook up but toilet seats?? Overall, our lives were good and "Project" living was comfortable, not extravagant but without want. Every Easter, we got new outfits and Christmas was always filled with gifts. As I said, daddy was a provider.

School for me was fun. I was not an "A" student just average. At that time, I was in the fifth grade, my goals were to be a crossing guard and wear the vinyl band and badge but at only four foot six, I never got a shot but I did make Eraser Monitor. Now many of you might not know what that was but an Eraser Monitor's job was to take the erasers outside and knock the chalk dust out of them. There really was not a rush to do this job so the short kid got to do it.

The school was PS8 in Brooklyn, walking distance

from the "Projects" and those walks to school remind me of the good times and good friends. One kid I remember, had a rough home life like me but his was abusive. Flynn Snead was his name and he lived on the second floor. His mom would beat his ass and the window would be open. You could hear Flynn hollering and his mom would beat him at the drop of a hat. She didn't give a damn who's hat it was. In a strange way, it gave me a little comfort to know I wasn't the only one with a secret home life; secret because we never let him know we heard the beatings. Life can often give you comfort simply by knowing "you're not the only one." In a way, it's like an antidepressant.

And during these early years, you used your mind to help you through those hard times. You make changes in your expectant goals. You see, when I realized, I did not make crossing guard, police officer was off my list. You see at these times, if there is nobody in your life to encourage you not to give up, you start to give up on goals and dreams. And so it begins to happen, the flow from goal to goal, dream to dream and you never really question why, just half ass accept what happened to you and move on with life and even opportunities.

Then another realization happened, you are confronted with how quickly life can end my relationship with the death of my friend James truly. On a warm summer day, a group of us are walking home from school back to the "Projects" chasing the girls with weeds that looked like cat. Then this tractor trailer driver saw us and he got out of his truck which he parked, turned over the sidewalk and started yelling at us. This did not go well with me and James. So James started throwing rocks at him. He went back in his truck, started to take off. James was under the rear wheels and he drove over him and crushed him to death. It was the first time I had seen someone killed and it was not a pretty sight. I ran all the way to my mom's job which at that time, she worked in the laundry of the YMCA which was next door to our building. I could hardly get the words out to tell her what I saw. James' death affected me. At this time, I thought death only came to old people. I'd never seen the life slowly leak from a person. James seemed to try and do a push up but could not so he slumped to the sidewalk and blood just spewed from his mouth and his life was over. We never played that game of chasing the girls again.

  I continued on at PS8 enjoying my friends who lived in the "Projects" doing all the things that kids do now. Family joined us. Cousin Bobby came along and he was kind of an idol to me. He was tall with a thick mustache and a great ball player. He soon met the best looking girl in the "Projects," April, and I had my first crush on a girl in Brooklyn. I tried to impress her by slicking down my curly hair but it was no use (laugh). She and Bobby later got married in the Church of the Open Door and as the years went by, I lost track of Bobby and his family. We only connected sometimes. At mama's house which was my father's mother, somehow our family never seemed to have that close bond like when I lived in Wilson. There was never alcohol. We were together just to be there for the pure love of family. I will suggest if your family gets to be like that, get together without alcohol every now and then because as I think back to those times, it helped to form a lot of my thoughts and actions into my teen and young adult years.

I did not mention this earlier but my grandmother was not just a hard worker but she was also a Reverend Minnie Oates who would sometimes take me to church with her. This, too, had an influence on me later in life: the music style hymn choir, no piano, no drums or anything like that - just a plain country church that you could hear foot stomping and singing a block before you got to church. At that time, I did not understand how deep this seed was planted in me because the world I had been moved to overwhelmed my life.

Our family carried on with the same lifestyle, occasionally, a trip to the beach at Coney Island which was always filled with highs and lows. In the morning, we would leave with sandwiches and chicken, Kool-Aid and of course the bottle of spirits. We would be good until the alcohol and sun set in. No fights but you talk about loud and noisy and somehow sand always got into the spice ham sandwiches but the trip home was always the worse. You see nobody owned a car so we all took the subway home, drunk, load and ashy. Nobody ever took lotion to the beach, so we all were pale gray on the train. I would try to sit away from the rest of the family but by the looks of my ashy skin, you could tell I was part of the Taylor clan (laugh). Then the walk from the subway to the "Projects" was the final blow in this beach trip until next year. So even today, I'm not crazy about the beach. My other disdain was the Boy's Club down the street. They would take the kids from the "Projects" to Ebbits Field to see the Brooklyn Dodgers play. The problem was we had to sit in the outfield seats that were not under a shelter. This section was called the bleachers due to the fact the sun would bleach your skin and the players looked like ants. We were so far away from the game. Even today, I don't go to baseball games.

    Now don't get me wrong, there were some good times living in the "Projects." I remember Louie Pilapin who lived in a home across from the "Projects." He would take me to church with him when he went to confession. To me, he went in this little box and talked to this guy then came out and got to the front of the church, kneeled down and say some "Hail Mary" stuff, then we would leave. Some days, we would go to the school part in the summer and the nuns would give us a peanut butter sandwich and an orange. He got me in trouble once by setting up a "hideout" in a cardboard box and built a fire to roast potatoes over. When I went home, my mother asked if I had been around that fire, I said "no," then she set my butt on fire (laugh).

Growing up in the "Projects" was quite a lesson for me. There were good times and things that left lifetime scars on me. As I grew up, I realized and recognized later in life, the beatings my mother got from my father and how it affected me. Now I don't want you to think that my mother was a saint. Every now and then she would leave Brooklyn and go over to Manhattan to visit my uncle that brought us up from the South. Now my Uncle Albert was a bartender and a pimp. When my mom went over to visit she would not get back until the next morning. My sister and I were home alone, I knowing a fight was coming and it always did. What amazed me was that my mother never left my father and she never even talked about leaving. I wondered was ass beatings just part of relationships or was that how a man kept a woman. Even to this day, I don't understand how a woman stays in an abusive relationship because if you whip my ass, I will run away for as long as I find something to step on (laugh).

Some of these fights really stick in my mind; one where my mother and father returned from a dance and went into their bedroom. Quietly, she sat down in a chair to take off her heals and while she was bent over, he kicked her in the mouth knocking out two of her front teeth. At that time, I mentally plotted to kill him. I was ten years old.

Then there was the time mother got even. The family was over for pigs' feet and greens. Daddy came home from his job at the docks. In the winter time, which it was, he was dressed in long johns and an extra pair of pants. He was also drunk so when he came in, he tried to impress his buddies that he ruled his woman. So he said something to mother who had taken a drink or two prior to his arrival. He did not like her answering him back so he slapped her. He did not know you ever slap a woman with a full pot of collard green water. When he slapped her, she poured that whole pot on him and with all that winter ware, he did not feel it right away but when he did, he took off. We lived on the ninth floor. He could not wait for the elevators, so he took off down the stairs. We looked out the window and when he got outside, steam was literally coming off his legs as he ran to Cumberland Hospital about five blocks away. I laughed and laughed. I've never seen a Negro run so fast and when you say smoking, he was smoking. Our house was quiet for the three weeks he had to remain in the bed. The burnt meat smell was awful but the peace was worth it. My mother's name became honey for those three weeks.

As I grew older, I went on to graduate from the 8th grade, on to high school and to meet more friends from all over Brooklyn. Now in that time, you were given a choice of three high schools. I chose Alexander Hamilton Vocation Tech because my best friend was going there. Afterwards, my best friend transferred to a boy's high school because it had a better reputation than Hamilton for sports. And I could not or was not allowed to transfer per my mother. So I stayed. Back in those days, a parent's word was law. Now days, kids show no fear and treat parents with no respect. Hamilton, as well as, Boy's high were all boy's school. My only interactions with girls happened on the walk from the Kingston Avenue train stop to school and after school at the Hoyt & Schemerhorn Station. After school, I wish I could tell some juicy stories about me and some girls but you see I was a virgin until well after high school. I was so shy, I would look and grin but that was as far as I would go with girls. My school partners would tease me. Once they asked me if I had ever tongue kissed and I said "hell no." I'm not lettin' a girl stick her tongue in my mouth. This was another time to ask. "What the hell happened to me?" One cause of this shyness, I was very short. I did not start to grow until after high school and girls were not interested in 4'8" guys.

Made in the USA
Columbia, SC
23 June 2023